World Tourism Organization

Market Intelligence and Promotion Section

Sustainable Development of Tourism Section

Madrid, February 2002

The Canadian
Ecotourism Market

Special Report, Number 15

Capitán Haya 42
28020 Madrid
Tel: (34) 91 567 81 00
Fax: (34) 91 571 37 33
E-mail: omt@world-tourism.org
Internet: www.world-tourism.org

The Canadian Ecotourism Market

ISBN: 92-844-0508-4

Published by the World Tourism Organization
Madrid, Spain

Printed by the World Tourism Organization. Madrid, Spain

Foreword

Background

In view of the sustained growth of tourism activity world-wide, it would be reasonable to assume that the ecotourism sector will develop along parallel lines. However, no extensive international market research has hitherto been conducted with a view to corroborating this hypothesis.

On the occasion of the designation by the United Nations of 2002 as the International Year of Ecotourism (IYE), the World Tourism Organization (WTO) has decided to undertake research with a view to increasing knowledge of the following seven countries in their capacity as ecotourism generating markets: Germany, USA, United Kingdom, Canada, Spain, France and Italy[1].

Market studies of this type must be based on a co-ordinated approach among the experts concerned, similar research methods and, more importantly, a common concept of the term «ecotourism» if they are to deliver well-founded conclusions and global recommendations. However, concepts of ecotourism clearly vary, not only from one country to another, but also within the same territory. Likewise, the specific attributes of each of the markets studied, the availability of tour operators to respond to surveys depending on whether they were run in peak or low seasons and the inclusion of ecotourism products in more general products do not permit a strict comparability of the different studies presented in this series of monographs.

Readers are therefore asked to consider the results of these studies as general trends relative to the ecotourism market, rather than absolute reference data. This is the first time that such researches have been initiated. These are pioneer studies, whose methodology and results can serve as basis for future researches in this topic.

---

[1] Another WTO publication, prepared with the technical contributions of its Member States, is also devoted to the IYE. This publication, titled as "Sustainable Development of Ecotourism: A Compilation of Good Practices" (ISBN: 92-844-0478-9), contains 55 case studies from 39 countries.

Aims, definitions and methodology

After briefly summarizing the general characteristics of tourism markets, these surveys set out to analyse and evaluate, in each of the aforementioned countries, the nature tourism and ecotourism generating market, its volume, characteristics, major trends and development prospects, consumer profiles, the role of the different marketing actors, product typologies and the main communication and marketing tools used in these markets.

It was with a view to meeting these aims that WTO hired seven experts – one per country – all of whom adopted similar research methods:

- gathering the results of existing research studies with the aim of making an initial appraisal of the volume of this market;

- running consumer surveys based on a single questionnaire for all countries with a view to studying demand trends;

- running surveys among tour operators whose policies and products are commensurate, to some extent at least, with ecotourism concepts;

- studying the catalogues and brochures put out by these tour operators;

- organizing tour operator discussion forums (or focus groups) on the occasion of tourism trade fairs with a view to comparing marketing methods and results, but also with the aim of discussing the very notion of ecotourism.

It should also be noted that the same definition of ecotourism was used by all the different experts. WTO has defined this activity at two levels:

1. **Nature tourism:** a form of tourism in which the main motivation is the observation and appreciation of nature.

2. **Ecotourism:** a form of tourism with the following characteristics:

   i. All nature-based forms of tourism in which the main motivation of the tourists is the observation and appreciation of nature as well as the traditional cultures prevailing in natural areas.

   ii. It contains educational and interpretation features.

   iii. It is generally, but not exclusively, organised for small groups by specialized and small locally-owned businesses. Foreign operators of varying sizes also organize, operate and/or market ecotourism tours, generally for small groups.

   iv. It minimizes negative impacts on the natural and socio-cultural environment.

v. It supports the protection of natural areas by:

- generating economic benefits for host communities, organizations and authorities that are responsible for conserving natural areas;

- creating jobs and income opportunities for local communities; and

- increasing awareness both among locals and tourists of the need to conserve natural and cultural assets.

The most outstanding results of the seven studies can be summed up as follows

1. The use of the term «ecotourism» in the marketing and promotional tools and used by tour operators is still relatively limited. It would appear that this term has not yet been integrated in the marketing strategies of the nature tourism sector.

2. Likewise, the tourism sector that most closely matches the concept of ecotourism represents a relatively small share of the market, an observation that is borne out by the small dimension of the tour operators that comprise this segment and the small number of tourists they cater for.

3. Conversely, these same tour operators apparently believe that the growth of ecotourism may outpace that of other tourism activities overall. Moreover, this growth appears to be consolidating irrespective of the destination considered. A priori, no world region appears to have a head-start although each region does have several landmark destinations.

4. The surveys conducted among the various audiences show that enthusiasm for nature tourism invariably goes hand-in-hand with a desire for meeting local communities and discovering different facets of their culture (gastronomy, handicrafts, customs, etc.).

5. According to tour operators, ecotourism enthusiasts are mostly people from relatively high social brackets and with relatively high levels of education; they are over 35 and women slightly outnumber men.

6. These studies also show that environmental awareness, while still in its infancy, is clearly growing.

7. As mentioned above, these initial findings must be confirmed on the basis of future studies. These preparatory surveys should nonetheless provide a springboard for a more in-depth examination of ecotourism markets, which will be one of the key elements of the World Ecotourism Summit to be held in Quebec, Canada, from 22 to 24 May 2002.

Acknowledgements

The World Tourism Organization would like to thank Mrs. Pam Wight of Pam Wight & Associates for the preparation of this report on behalf of WTO.

The World Tourism Organization and the authors would like to express their gratitude to all those tour operators who generously lent their time to participate in this research through the questionnaire survey and the tour operators focus groups in Toronto and Montreal. They are also grateful to the tourists who participated in the ecotourist focus group.

Research for this report was undertaken by a team of Canadian experts commissioned by the World Tourism Organization, under the supervision of Mr. Eugenio Yunis, Chief, Sustainable Development of Tourism, WTO and Mr. Augusto Huescar, Chief, Market Intelligence and Promotion Section, WTO.
Mr. Philippe Lemaistre, Programme Officer at WTO, reviewed draft texts, tables and final editing of the report..

Table of Contents

Executive Summary

As part of the preparatory activities for the International Year of Ecotourism, the World Tourism Organization (WTO) commissioned a series of country studies, of which this study of Canadian outbound ecotourists is one. The study uses a variety of primary and secondary research to examine independent ecotourists as well as tour operator markets.

The WTO definitions of ecotourism and nature tourism are used, and almost all of those surveyed and in focus groups agreed with the definitions. However, only about half the tour operators who offer ecotourism product use the word ecotourism in the marketing. They feel that there is a lot of confusion in the marketplace and among other operators about definitions.

Canadians are very interested in nature, but mainly travel within Canada for their vacations, including nature/ecotourism. The US is the most popular outbound destination, but international travel has grown far more steadily than US travel, to a current peak of about 4.5 million travellers to international (non-US). Seniors comprise the most important segment for international travel, both independently and as group tour markets. Tour operators have seen high growth rates internationally, and expect this to continue. In this study, visiting parks is used as a proxy for nature tourism. It is interesting that visiting parks increases in importance the further from home. Thus, 10% of domestic trips include parks, 20% of US trips, and 40% of international trips. Visiting parks has steadily doubled over the last 15 years, indicating the interest in nature tourism.

Canada's outbound ecotourism operators many focus on nature/ecotourism, or handle other types of tourism, but the more a company focuses on nature/ecotourism, the smaller the average number of clients per firm is likely to be. Not only are their general tourism markets growing, but their ecotourism markets are growing also (29% growth over the last few years). Almost all operators expect this growth in nature/ecotourism markets to continue.

Canadian ecotourists may be considered independent travellers or group travellers. Sometimes the two groups share characteristics and preferences, sometimes there are differences. The typical Canadian ecotourist tends to be: of any age, equally likely to be male or female, from a higher income household, and highly educated, likely with college training. The independent travellers are more likely to be younger, especially 25 to 54, while the group travellers tend to be older, especially 45 to 74.

The household composition is mainly couples, or couples with children. Party composition varies slightly –independent ecotourists tend to be mainly families with children, then couples, whereas tour groups tend to be mainly single, then couples.

The ecotourism trip is generally part of a more classic vacation, for tour groups and especially for independent travellers. For tour operators, the most popular package vacation length tends to be 2 weeks, whereas for the independent travellers, the preferred trip length is somewhat longer, from 8 days to over 2 weeks. These independent travellers take multiple trips per year, of which 1 in 3 international trips are likely to involve ecotourism. All ecotourists would prefer the summer for vacation travel, but there is actually interest in all seasons.

Both the ecotourists and the tour operators are conscious of the need to concern themselves with the destination – conservation activities as well as community development opportunities. Tour operators tend to give priority to hiring locally, especially local guides, whom they consider extremely important to the success of their programs. They also may engage in local partnerships or support programs. Half of the operators encourage their clients to donate to projects in the destinations, whether money or time or physical assistance. Ecotourists feel tour operators should be involved in activities, which benefit the destinations (conservation or community development), more than they think they themselves should be involved in such activities. However, approximately half the ecotourists donate money to charitable or conservation causes and projects.

The willingness to pay for an ecotourism vacation varies tremendously; however, the most popular tour operator packages are priced between $2,000 and $5,000 (44%). Over a quarter of ecotourists is willing to pay between $1,500 and $3,000 for an ecotourism trip, and 11% would pay over $3,000. They would also be prepared to pay a little more for a vacation, which benefited the environment.

Trends which continue to influence the industry, or which have emerged recently include: a continued increase in ecotourism itself, increase education travel, continued growth in soft adventure, concerns about the environment, awards or recognition for environmental activities, conservation vacations, more small group travel, and increasing interest in culture along with the environment.

The destinations which are most important for Canadians overall, include the UK, Mexico, France, and Cuba. Most Canadians are interested in Canada for their next ecotourism trip, but 20% are interested in international destinations. Those destinations, which attract ecotourists, cover virtually all continents and regions, except the CIS Countries, with the main destinations being Latin/Central America, Asia, and Africa. It is interesting, too, that tour operators indicate that exotic (e.g., Mongolia) or "trophy" (e.g., Galapagos) destinations are of appeal to their markets.

While scenery is the most important reason for a trip, motivations of importance are: the desire for new experiences (29%), as well as the desire to return to a familiar or satisfying place (20%). The activities, which are most popular by independent and group ecotourists are hiking, camping and walking. Preferred accommodation still tends to be conventional hotels and motels, but there is a move to select other types of accommodation, which are more representative of the overall experience. The experiences sought by independent ecotourists are experiencing wilderness, interpretive/learning experiences, and discovering local cultures and foods. The experiences sought by tour operators are knowledgeable guides, interpretive/learning experiences, and wildlife viewing.

Planning times before trips tend to be relatively short – generally less than 3 months – and independent ecotourists prefer to make their travel arrangements themselves. Both tour operators and independent ecotourists indicate that word of mouth is the most important means for markets to decide where to go, and with whom. Word of mouth may include friends, relatives, or others. The implications for tour operators are that the experiences they provide should be extremely satisfying, particularly since "personal experiences" are one more reason for selecting a destination or operator. Ecotourists do a considerable amount of research before a trip, particularly via the Internet, friends, and they use travel brochures, books and specialist magazines. They are also twice as likely as the general public to belong to organisations.

Although Canada itself is the main destination, Canadian ecotourism appears to be growing, including to international destinations. While independent ecotourists sometimes have different characteristics and preferences than group tour markets, often their characteristics and preferences are similar. The use of the information, which follows, should be helpful both for tour operators and for potential destinations for Canadian ecotourists.

1. Introduction

1.1 Purpose of the Study

Recognising the increasing global importance of ecotourism, the United Nations designated the year 2002 as the International Year of Ecotourism, and its Commission on Sustainable Development requested international agencies, governments and the private sector to undertake supportive activities. The World Tourism Organization (WTO) has joined forces with the United Nations Environment Programme (UNEP) to take a leading role in the preparation and co-ordination of activities to be undertaken at the international level during the IYE.

In anticipation thereof, seven studies have been commissioned by the World Tourism Organization in Germany, Great Britain, Italy, Canada, the United States of America, France and Spain to analyse the ecotourism market in each country.

The current study is intended to provide an analysis of ecotourism markets in Canada, and to determine the relative importance of ecotourism in Canada's tourism marketplace, focussing on outbound ecotourism. A key objective was to better understand ecotourism market characteristics, motivations and relationship with commercial suppliers, as well as market size, and how well the definition of ecotourism is both understood and accepted.

1.2 Territorial Coverage

This report focuses on Canada – whether focussing on the population of Canadians who form the ecotourism marketplace, or the tour operators and agencies which are based/headquartered in Canada.

By contrast, the ecotourism destinations presented and discussed may include the whole world, including Canada, but with a focus on overseas destinations.

1.3 Definition of Ecotourism in the Context of this Study

The definitions used in this report are those used by the WTO, and adapted from the findings of a WTO multistakeholder working group, which distinguished between sustainable tourism and ecotourism. This group indicated that:

Ecotourism is a form of tourism that is practised in relatively undisturbed natural areas, for the main purposes of admiring them and learning more about their habitats; intrinsic to this definition is the need for ecotourism operations to reduce to a minimum and if possible avoid its impacts on the area visited. Furthermore, ecotourism must contribute to the conservation of natural areas and the sustainable development of adjacent areas and communities, and it should generate further environmental and conservation awareness among resident populations and visitors. March 2000, Madrid.

For the survey materials and focus group discussions, the WTO definitions were summarised:

Nature Tourism

"All types of tourism based on nature, where the primary motivation of tourists is the observation and appreciation of nature, as well as cultures".

Ecotourism

"Ecotourism goes beyond nature tourism, and occurs in relatively undisturbed natural areas, for the main purpose of admiring them and learning more about them. Ecotourism implies that the tour operator and the visitors will have some responsibility towards the destination, reducing or avoiding impacts on the areas visited. Ecotourism should contribute to conservation of the natural areas, and contribute local economic benefits, as well as generating awareness of conservation among residents and visitors."

For certain study components, the definitions were explained more fully. For example, in the Tour Operator Survey, the following explanation was provided:

In practical terms, ecotourism products should consist of the following:

a. Include educational or interpretive aspects related to nature

b. Consist of small groups

c. Minimise negative impacts on the natural and cultural environments

d. *Contribute to the protection of natural areas by:*

- *generating economic benefit for locals;*

- *employing locally;*

- *increasing locals/visitors awareness of the need for environmental and cultural protection.*

For the purposes of this study, both nature-based tourism and ecotourism were included, but differentiated. However, all respondents were asked to discuss the WTO definitions and to elaborate or explain their reaction. In particular, the ecotourist and tour operator focus groups yielded helpful information and perspectives. This information is summarised in Appendix A: Canadian Perspectives on Definitions.

1.4 Research Methodology

In order to develop this report, this study was conducted in the following ways:

1. *Review and compilation of existing literature and studies of the Canadian ecotourism market*

A number of studies have examined ecotourism in Canada. These were used as references, and are listed in the bibliography.

2. *Ecotourist focus group*

In order to discuss the issues particular to this project, a focus group was convened with 13 mixed members of the public who had travelled abroad on a trip that involved experiencing and learning about nature and the environment – i.e., an ecotourism trip in another country. The results of a focus group cannot be extrapolated to all outbound Canadian ecotourists; however, they were used to support other findings in this report. In addition, where information was unavailable from other sources, focus group findings were used (e.g., to evaluate ecotourists' commitment to the destination, conservation and community development objectives).

3. *Synopsis of previous surveys of Canadian ecotourists*

While previous studies of ecotourism in Canada have examined markets, most focus on inbound markets. One survey (HLA/ARA 1994) examined North American ecotourists, which included a Canadian component. This was the first global survey of ecotourists. Another survey (Eagles and Cascagnette, 1993) examined

Canadian ecotourists. Yet, another study examined Canadian markets interested in ecotourism in Ontario (Twynam and Robinson, 1997), but its findings complement the other surveys. These major surveys of Canadians, together with special runs of Statistics Canada surveys and data mining of previous surveys were used to confirm report findings. Their summarised results can be found in Appendix E – Canadian Surveys: Summarised Results.

4. *Data mining of the Canadian component of previous North American ecotourist surveys*

The HLA/ARA study (1994) surveyed 7 major metropolitan areas, including two in Canada. Almost 400 Canadians were surveyed (from higher than average income neighbourhoods in Toronto [193] and Winnipeg [200] – these were neighbourhoods of over $45,000 average household incomes). All respondents had a strong propensity to travel, and represent "nature tourism" markets, since they had all either taken or were interested in taking a vacation that involved nature, adventure, or culture in the countryside or wilderness. The questionnaire is found in Appendix B: Survey Instrument.

In order to refine the information available about such nature tourism markets, and to focus on the "purer" ecotourist sample, the data were specially run so as to focus on a core group. This was done using one question of the survey (#3i), which asked respondents to rate the importance of 15 different activities and services. The following of the 15 elements were considered to be have most affinity with those which ecotourists might be expected to feel important.

- a wilderness setting

- visiting a national park or other protected area

- interpretive educational programs

- the importance of guides

- viewing wildlife

All respondents who rated at least two of these elements as "very important" (on a 5-point Likert scale) were included in the special data runs conducted for the WTO project. This resulted in 120 "purer ecotourists". The findings are presented in the comparative tables in various sections throughout this report as Canadian Ecotourists, referenced as "special runs of 1994 survey data".

5. *Special runs of Statistics Canada surveys of Canadians on outbound travel*

There are currently no surveys, which measure ecotourism movements to, and from Canada, thus it is not possible to accurately measure the volume of eco-tourists from Canada. However, an approximation of markets interested in nature-based experiences can be inferred from Statistics Canada surveys of Canadians who travel internationally and indicate an interest in relevant activities. The closest activity category to ecotourists is *those who visited a national, provincial, or regional park or historic site.*

In 2000, Statistics Canada sampled Canadians who travelled outside the country to the US and other international locations. The total number of person-trips outside Canada was 5,349,800. Of these, 61% were to the US, and 39% were to other overseas destinations. Conventionally, Canadian statistics separate US data from other international data, because the numbers related to the US are so high. The WTO is interested in international destinations for the purposes of the current study. Thus the information which was disaggregated for this study represents weighted data of Canadians who visited a National, Provincial, Regional Park or Historic site and who made trips to overseas destinations (rather than to the US). This information is found in the comparative tables in various sections throughout this report, referenced as Statistics Canada, 2001.

6. *Tour Operators Survey*

A long list was compiled of Canadian tour operators, who handled Canadian clients. The names were obtained from various sources, including the Communiqué (a Canadian Tourism Commission [CTC] publication); CTX (a CTC web-based industry information source); a previous study of Canadian ecotourism tour operators (Pam Wight & Associates, 1999); correspondence with those who compile databases of ecotourism operators (GONOMAD travel); and a guide to Canada's travel industry (Baxter Publishing 2000). These sources yielded hundreds of companies, of which many could be removed, because they were known not to deal with outbound, and not to deal with nature tourism or ecotourism.

A long list of companies was contacted, to screen them, so as to fit the WTO criteria (i.e., outbound operators, with some portion of their product being *nature tourism or ecotourism*). They were sent a cover letter, explaining the project, and the WTO criteria, and the benefits of participation. Over 100 companies were contacted by phone and email. Several waves of contact were made over 3 months, both by phone and by email, to maximise response from those companies. Many companies excluded themselves on the basis of being inbound, or not dealing with nature or ecotourism, or for other reasons. A total of 29 responses were obtained, which is a very fair representation of outbound Canadian operators dealing with ecotourism/nature tourism in Canada. These are listed in Appendix C: Tour Operators responding to the Survey. The survey instrument is presented in Appendix F: Tour Operator Survey.

7. An analysis of tour operator web-sites, brochures and catalogues

Screening for outbound operators involved in ecotourism or nature travel was done prior to the tour operator survey by telephone and email. Once those operators involved in nature or ecotourism were determined, the materials used for communications with their markets were analysed. These included web-sites, catalogues, brochures, and other materials. There was not a high response to our request for brochures and other written materials. One of the principal reasons for the analysis was to examine the use of the words "ecotourism" and "nature tourism", as well as to provide any supplementary information about products, group size, conservation benefits, local community benefits, and market messages.

8. Tour Operators Focus Groups

In order to have more in-depth feedback from the tour operator market, two focus groups were held in Toronto and Montreal, to represent the English and French speaking markets of the largest travel centres in Canada. These were held with 29 operators listed in Appendix D: Tour Operator Focus Group Participants. The purpose of the focus groups was to find out detailed information about their markets and products, and to identify ecotourism market and operators' preferences with respect to destinations and services, amenities and features, as well as to estimate the volume of their business provided by ecotourism and nature tourism markets.

2. The Global Tourism Market in Canada

2.1 Historical Growth (1986 – 2000)

Canada has been a significant origin country for both domestic travel and travel to other countries. Statistics Canada is the main source of information, and provides good quality information on travel domestically, to the US and internationally[2].

The most important travel destination for Canadians is Canada. In 1999, more than 93.9 million overnight trips were taken to and within Canada, a 10% rise over the previous year. Canadians accounted for the bulk of trips and revenues (79%). They embarked on 74.6 million trips across the country, up slightly over 1998. Almost half the travel by Canadians was taken by residents of Ontario (26 million overnight visits). Also significant were Quebec (16 million) and British Columbia (10 million). Although Canadians accounted for 79% of the trips, they only accounted for 58% of the expenditures (the international visitors made 42% of expenditures although they were made 21% of overnight visits).

The top 10 activities that Canadians prefer while travelling in Canada are listed below (Statistics Canada and CTC 1999):

1. Shopping	**6. Visit National, provincial or regional park, or historic site**
2. Sightseeing	7. Visit zoo, museum or natural display
3. Going to a sports/outdoor activities	8. Attending cultural event
4. Visit friends or relatives	9. Attending a festival/fair/exhibition
5. Going to a bar or night club	10. Visit theme park

---

2 It should be noted that Canada and the US share many market characteristics and preferences. Crossing the US border if is relatively easy for Canadians, and the two countries share the longest undefended border, globally. The US is both Canada's largest origin market and its largest destination for travellers. In many Canadian travel statistics, the breakdown is for Canada, the US, and international. For the purpose of the WTO study, it is the destinations other than Canada or the US which are of interest, thus it is the international component (rather than the US) which is the main focus in most of this report, where by "international" we mean countries other than the US, unless stated otherwise.

The top activity is shopping, with over one third of Canadians participating. The category of visiting National, Provincial or Regional Parks, or Historic Sites is highlighted because this is the activity category that is most likely to be of interest to nature tourists or ecotourists. It is the 6th most popular category of activity, and had about 10% of inter-provincial travellers participating.

The US has always been the most popular destination for Canadian outbound travellers, accounting for most (91%) overnight trips. The top 10 US states visited are:

1. New York	6. Nevada
2. Florida	7. Maine
3. Washington	8. Pennsylvania
4. Michigan	9. Vermont
5. California	10. Ohio

Figure 2.1 shows the portion of Canadians travelling to total international destinations (including the US) over the last 15 years, and it also shows total international travel separate from US travel. It is very evident that the US is the major influence on total numbers.

Total international travel increased over the 15 years period from about 40 million to almost 50 million travellers. However, there were peaks during this period – the total numbers increased constantly from 1985 to 1991, then began to shrink. However, the decrease was for visits to the US; **visits to overseas destinations has actually increased significantly (virtually doubled) from 1986 to the present.**

For example, in 1986, just over 2 million Canadians went to countries other than the US (2,285,000) but by 2000 there were almost 5 million international visitors (4,516,000). The relative percentage of overseas travel has increased, too, from almost 6% in 1986, to almost 10% in 2000.

Figure 2.1: Canadian International Travel: Total, and International (excluding US)

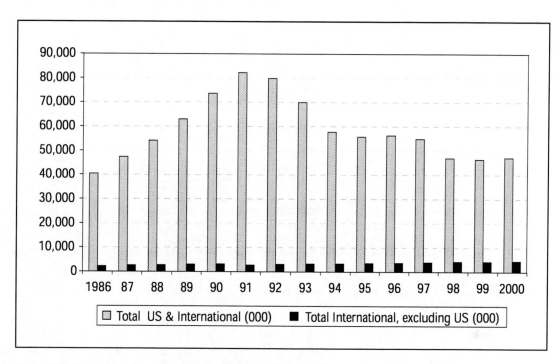

Source: Statistics Canada and Canadian Tourism Commission, 1999.

Also, during this period, the *length* of trips changed, with the proportion of longer trips (over 3 weeks) decreasing, and the proportion of medium-length trips (7-13 days) increasing. Over this period, the amount of *spending has also increased*. The following text focuses on international travel by Canadians (i.e., to destinations excluding the US).

Europe has always been the most popular international region for Canadian travellers, with 6 European countries in Canada's top 10 destination list, and Britain continues to stay at the top of the list (Figure 2.2). Switzerland is the country that has shown the greatest decline in visitation. Although many of the countries have remained at much the same level of popularity, over this period the Caribbean has grown significantly in popularity, especially Cuba and the Dominican Republic. Mexico is very notable (as a non-European destination) in having consistently remained as the 2nd or 3rd most popular destination overall for Canadians travelling internationally.

Figure 2.2: Top 10 Overseas Countries Visited by Canadians (Overnight Visitors)

1986	1991	1996	1999[1]
UK	UK	UK	UK
France	Mexico	Mexico	Mexico +
Mexico	France	France	France -
W. Germany	Germany	Germany	Cuba ++
Netherlands	Netherlands	Cuba	Germany -
Switzerland	Cuba	Italy	Italy +
Italy	Dominican Republic	Netherlands	Netherlands -
Australia	Italy	Hong Kong	Dominican Republic
Jamaica	Switzerland	Switzerland	Hong Kong +
Dominican Republic	Hong Kong	Dominican Republic	Switzerland —

1. Symbols are used to provide an idea of relative change, using the actual visitation numbers:

   + = increase; ++ = strong increase; - = decrease; — = stronger decrease

Source: Statistics Canada and Canadian Tourism Commission, 1999.

The most popular activities for Canadians travelling internationally are listed below, and are similar in rank (although not in percentage) to domestic activity preferences (Statistics Canada and CTC 1999).

1. Shopping	**6. Visit National, provincial or regional park, or historic site**
2. Sightseeing	7. Visit zoo, museum or natural display
3. Going to a sports/outdoor activities	8. Attending cultural event
4. Visit friends or relatives	9. Attending a festival/fair/exhibition
5. Going to a bar or night club	10. Visit theme park

Over three quarters of Canadians engage in shopping and sightseeing while abroad (77%), but visiting national, provincial or regional parks or historic sites are bolded, because these activities are most likely to represent activities of interest to eco-tourists or nature tourists, and **40% of Canadians travelling internationally visit parks or historic sites.**

2.2 Current Trends – Qualitative and Quantitative

General Canadian' International Travel Trends

A number of Canadian travel trends have been observed for the 1990s (McDougall 1999) including those related to age, family structure, and international travel. The importance of the seniors market (defined as over 65) is particularly highlighted. These trends are:

- **The growth in domestic and international trips by seniors over the past decade has outpaced most age groups**, particularly for international travel

- Seniors tend to take longer trips, especially during winter, and are more likely to travel alone

- Seniors are more likely to travel in the off-season when travelling to an international destination

- Senior women travellers outnumber men by a ratio of 58 to 42 to the US, and 56 to 44 for overseas destinations

- Travel propensity to overseas countries is most prevalent among those aged 55 to 64 (10%), then decreases to 7% among seniors

- In terms of propensity to travel, those ages most likely to travel internationally are 55-64 (10%), 45-54 (9%), 15-24 (8%)

- Europe was the most popular destination for seniors – the UK led (22% of trips), followed by Mexico (7%), France (5%), Germany (5%), Netherlands (4%), and Italy (4%)

In addition, over the decade, the gap in the number of trips per 100 residents has widened between younger adults (20-44 years) and older adults (45+). Thus, **over the last decade, international travel has become less attractive, relatively, to young adults, and more attractive and affordable to older adults**.

Further observations were made by Shaienks (2000) related to family structure and travel:

- In 1998, 79% of all trips, and 88% of expenditures by Canadians were made by adults travelling without children.

- The US was the first choice for 85% of Canadians; 15% went overseas

- Adults travelling alone chose an overseas destination more often (nearly 25% of the time)

- **Overseas trips were longer** (nearly 17 nights overseas, 6 nights US) for families; and even longer for adults travelling alone (18 nights overseas and 9 nights US)

- Expenditures per trip were greater for overseas than the US (although families spend about the same amount whether US or overseas-bound, while adults without children spend slightly more per day overseas)

- **Activities of interest are similar whether travelling in Canada or abroad.** The participation rate is higher for families than adults travelling without children. **The one exception is visiting parks and historic sites.**

- **Interest in parks is higher the further Canadians go from home** (3% intra-provincial, 10% inter-provincial, 20% US travel, 40% International travel)

Trends in Group Travel

The trends over the *last* few years for tour operators surveyed for this project, has generally been very positive with respect to the total number of clients. While a very small number experienced a decline in total clients, almost all tour operators reported a growth in the total number of clients. The rate of growth of their markets varied, but was spread from about a 5-10% growth rate for a few operators, to those operators where client numbers had almost doubled over the last few years.

The average growth rate presented by operators was:

- **35% growth rate for total tour operator product offerings**

2.3 Expected Growth in Outbound Tourism

General Canadians' International Travel Potential

In the summer of 2001, a Conference Board of Canada survey found that the short-term outlook for travel *to the US* by Canadians would be at an all time low, although this was expected to improve over time. In addition, airlines were rated much lower than many other travel industry sector categories. Further, as the Canadian dollar depreciates, Canadians are inclined to make fewer visits to the US. Similarly, a decline in the growth of real disposable income will result in fewer international visits, as Canadians cut back on discretionary spending.

With the recent upheavals in the travel industry following the September 11th terrorism attack in the US, this downturn in US travel may be greatly exacerbated over the short and medium term. International travel is extremely volatile (less so for travel to the US), and is influenced by non-economic factors, such as wars, terrorism, special events, regulation (e.g. visa requirements) and capacity. Sometimes such non-economic factors exert more influence on travel behaviour than any of the economic factors in conventional models. An October 2001 survey showed that only 28% of Canadians interviewed believe they will reduce their air travel in the next two years due to terrorism, compared with 48% in the US (Davis 2001). However, this would still be a significant reduction on Canadian travel. There is therefore likely to be a negative impact on Canadians' international travel, due to security concerns, in the short to medium term.

However, over the longer term, Canadians' interest in international travel looks positive. If one looks at the growth over the last 15 years, international travel has increased steadily every year. Over the long term, such growth in international travel is likely to continue.

- **If doubling of international travel occurs in the next 15 years, we could expect approximately 9 million international trips in the year 2015.**

Group Travel Futures

Tour operators surveyed in the course of this project were asked about the expected future in their tourism markets overall. Only one anticipated a decline in markets, 2 anticipated markets to stay the same, and all other respondents (25) anticipated a growth in their total markets.

Growth p.a. over last 3 years	
Decline in Clients	2
Staying the same	–
"growing"	7
0-5%	1
6-10%	2
11-19%	4
20-34%	2
35-49%	2
50-74%	4
75-100%	2

(Source: TO survey, 2001)

The trends over the last few years for tour operators surveyed for this project, has generally been very positive with respect to both the total number of clients and with respect to nature/ecotourism clients.

- If one assumes that the growth rate for the future is the same as the growth rate that tour operators stated for the past 3 years, one could project growth of **up to 35% for *total* product offerings.**

2.4 Conclusions

- Canada is the most important travel destination for Canadians

- The US is the most popular destinations for outbound Canadians

- Overseas (non-US) travel has increased steadily over the last 15 years, from about 2.3 million to almost 4.5 million travellers

- Top overseas destinations are, in order of magnitude: UK, Mexico, France and Cuba, the latter showing the most dramatic increase

- The seniors market is important and growing for international travel

- Group travel has grown at an average rate of 35% for operators surveyed

- At the current rate of increase, travel abroad (non-US) is likely to almost double in the next 15 years

- Tour operators anticipate markets to grow over the next few years, possibly by up to 35%

3. The Ecotourism Market in Canada

3.1 Quantitative Demand by Canadians

Canada currently does not measure ecotourist travel. Thus, studies, which directly measure market volume and potential, do not exist. The variety of definitions of ecotourism also presents a problem. It is paradoxical that the more precise the definition of ecotourists, and the more that definition includes *motivational* characteristics, the greater the difficulty in measuring the volume of ecotourists, because most exit survey instruments ask about more tangible aspects of trip, such as type of activities, attractions, or expenditures. Some such questions may *indirectly* indicate the volume of markets likely to be interested in ecotourism. But only very occasional, one-off surveys ask information about motivational elements, and these are usually *inbound* rather than outbound surveys.

The WTO definition includes motivational characteristics. Thus this report cannot provide numbers of ecotourists according to such a definition. Nor can this report plot the growth of Canadian ecotourists, for the same reasons. Canada does, however, have exit surveys of travellers, which may assist in indicating the volume of ecotourists. Also, there have been other studies done on ecotourism market potential, which allow indirect conclusions to be made about ecotourism potential, and which are used here.

3.1.1 Domestic Markets

A number of domestic studies reveal that Canadians are interested in nature and ecotourism. Key findings from these studies include information related to Nature tourism and Ecotourism.

Interest in Nature Tourism in Canada by Canadians

There have been studies led by Statistics Canada, approximately every 5 years, of the Importance of Wildlife or Nature, to Canadians (Environment Canada, 2001). This is a comprehensive survey of about 87,000 Canadians 15 years of age and over. Key findings include:

1991

- **In 1991, nearly one in five Canadians (18.7%)** took special trips away from their homes in order to watch, photograph, feed, or study wildlife. They devoted a total of 84.3 million days to these trips, or an average of 22 days per participant, and spent $2.4 billion on travel expenses and special equipment for these trips. There were 3.8 million primary non-consumptive wildlife trips

- **Since 1981, there has been substantial growth in the number of participants and in the amount of leisure time spent on wildlife-related activities since similar surveys** (in 1981 and 1987). This reveals the growing importance of these activities to Canadians. **Total expenditures on wildlife-related activities increased by 32.9 percent between 1981 and 1991**

1996

- **In 1996, nearly one in five Canadians (18.6%)** over age 15 participated in wildlife viewing in Canada (4.4 million Canadians). Of these, 1.5 million have wildlife viewing as their *main* activity. This was most popular among Canadians between the ages of 20 and 25, particularly 25 to 44 year old, and for those with higher than average education.

- **20 million Canadians, aged 15 and over, took part in one or more nature-related activities in Canada.** They took 191 million trips, of which a quarter was overnight trips to enjoy nature-related activities.

- Almost half of Canadians participated in one or more of 17 specified outdoor activities in natural areas in Canada (e.g., sightseeing, camping, photographing, gathering, swimming, canoeing/boating, hiking, etc.). **Over half the participants visited national or provincial parks or other protected areas for these activities.**

In 1996, for those who had wildlife viewing as the *main* activity in their trip (1.5 million), the following is of relevance:

- 83.1% *watched* wildlife

- 45.8% *photographed* wildlife

- 42.0% *studied* wildlife

- 24.9% *fed* wildlife

- 12.7% took trips to other provinces/territories to view wildlife

- **50.8% took trips to national or provincial parks or other protected areas for the main reason of viewing wildlife**

The conclusions which may be drawn from this substantive survey of Canadians, in terms of quantitative demand for ecotourism-related products follow:

Canadian Population 2000	30,750,087
Population aged 15 and over (80.9%)	24,879,199
18.6% of Canadians aged 15+ participate in Wildlife viewing	**4,627,531**
Approx. 1/2 of Canadians 15+ participate in a range of outdoor activities (sightseeing, camping, photographing, gathering, swimming, canoeing/boating, hiking, etc)	~12.4 million
Just over 1/2 of these participants in outdoor activities had visited a park or protected area for these activities (24.9% of those 15+)	**~6.2 million**

- **It is reasonable to assume from these figures that between 18% and 24% of Canadians over age 15 (or 15% to 20% of Canadians) are interested in ecotourism-related activities.**

3.1.2 International Travellers

Statistics Canada surveys Canadians returning from US and International travel. It was found that 20% of visitors to the US visit national or other parks and historic sites, but that that number increases to 40% for international travellers. The demand for nature-based activities can be approximated by looking at those interested in visiting parks (Figure 3.1). The total, for the last few years, has been around 10 million trips by this group. This group should be taken to have some interest in nature, but by no means to be equated with nature tourists, whose numbers would be somewhat less than this.

For this group (international visitors, not US visitors):

- average party size is 1.95
- average trip length (nights) is 18.35
- average trip spending is $1,671.83
- average daily expenditures is $91.12

- **Interest in international (non-US) trips has increased steadily (doubled) over the last 15 years, going from 2.3 million in 1996, to 4.5 million in 2000, with trips to parks (nature tourism) also doubling in that time (0.9 million to 1.8 million in 2000).**

Figure 3.1: Canadians Visiting National or Other Parks or Historic Sites (US and overseas Trips)

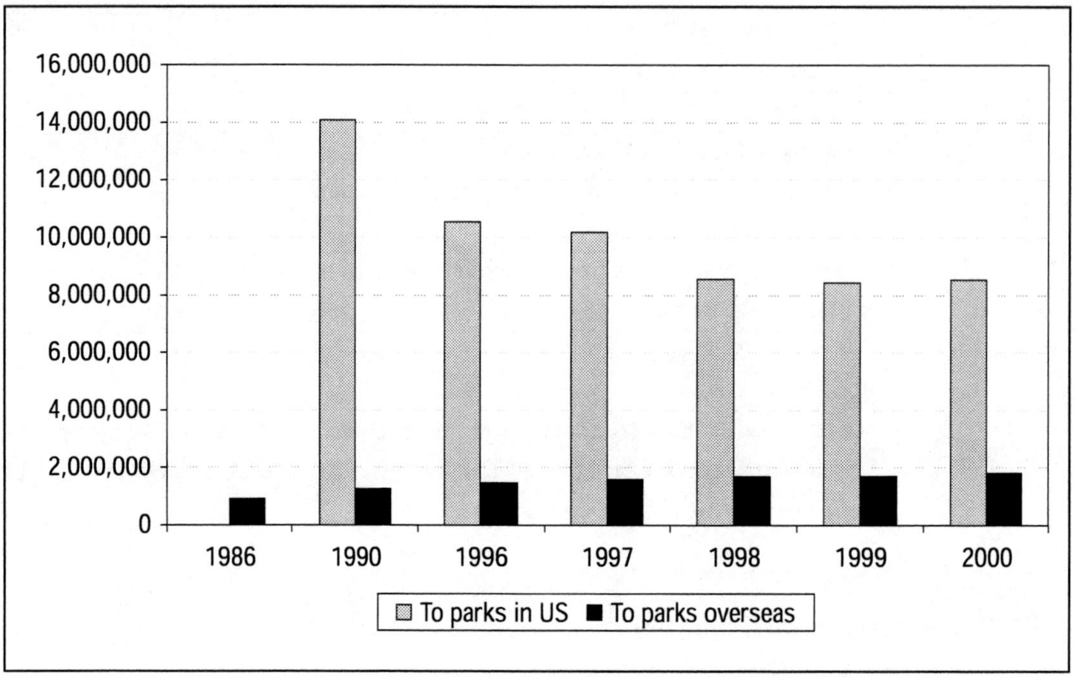

Source: Statistics Canada 2001

3.2 Estimates of Canadian Markets: Package and Independent

Estimate of Tour Operator Markets

As part of this project, most Canadian outbound operators who had ecotourism or nature tourism products were surveyed. Of the 29 companies surveyed, 19 indicated their approximate *total* number of clients, per year, and 14 indicated the number of *nature/ecotourism clients* (Table 3.1). This does not represent the *total* number of commercially facilitated outbound Canadian nature/ecotourists; however, it represents a very significant portion of them. It should also be noted that *inbound* operators were not targeted for the survey, and a considerable number of Canadians travel *within* Canada for ecotourism experiences, and domestic travellers represent the greatest proportion of both general travellers, and nature/ecotourists.

Also, outbound companies may deal with as few as 5% Canadians in their total client base, or as many as 100% Canadians. So it is not possible to make accurate calculations of the outbound Canadian nature/ecotourism market channelled via tour operators. However, the findings certainly provide good indications of volume and characteristics of outbound Canadian tour markets.

Table 3.1: Size of Total Client Base and Nature/Ecotourism Client Base

Total Clients	Total Clients	Nature/ Ecotourism Clients
100 or less	2	4
101 – 300	3	2
301 – 750	5	2
751 – 1,250	2	2
1,251 – 2,000	1	1
2,001 – 3,500	2	0
3,501 – 7,500	3	3
Over 7,500	1	0
Total Respondents	**19**	**14**

TO Survey, 2001

Nature or ecotourism products occupy a varying degree of importance as a percentage of business, for each company. Only 27 companies provided this breakdown of business between their nature and ecotourism volume of business (Table 3.2). For many companies, nature/ecotourism represents their *total* volume of business, whereas for others, nature and ecotourism components are only *small* parts of their total business.

Most significant is the fact that while there was a spread of total clients, ranging from around 100 clients per year to over 7,500, there was less of a spread for nature/ecotourism clients. Most companies (10 of 14) had fewer than 1,250 clients annually, and most were in the 100-750-client size range (Table 3.1).

Table 3.2: Companies Reporting the Size (%) of the Nature and Ecotourism Portions of their Business

% of Company Operations	Nature Tourism Component (No. of Operators)	Ecotourism Component (No. of Operators)
0-9%	5	6
10-20%	6	5
21-35%	1	1
36-50%	3	2
51-75%	1	1
76-100%	11	11
Total Respondents	**27**	**27**

TO Survey, 2001

One of the interesting findings is that operators tend to feel either, that their operation is strongly focussed towards either ecotourism *or* to nature tourism – there are few operators in the middle ranges (i.e., few where each type of product is approximately 50:50 of operations).

Tour operators were asked to provide their total number of clients, as well as the numbers who took nature/ecotourism trips. Of those who responded, the results are shown in Table 3.3.

Many companies felt that providing actual numbers of clients was proprietary information. This table, therefore, presents the responding companies (18). They have been grouped into those companies with over 50% of their total number of clients being nature/ecotourism clients (in every case, this was 100% of the client base for the 11 companies in this category); and those companies with fewer than 50% of clients interested in nature/ecotourism. The total number of clients and the total number of nature/ecotourism clients are actual totals from the figures provided by each company, and were used to provide the average numbers of clients per firm, and the average numbers of nature/ecotourists per firm. This information was then used to make deductions about those companies, which did not provide any client numbers.

Table 3.3: Numbers of Clients Served by Operators[1]

Specialisation in Nature/ Ecotourism	No. of Respondents	Total Clients	Total Clients per Firm, on Av.	% Nature/ Ecotourism Clients	Total Nature/ Ecotourism Clients	Nature/ Ecotourism Clients per Firm, on Av.
> 50% of clients seeking nature/ ecotourism	11	21,770	1,979 (ranges from 100 to 6,500)	100%	21,770	1,979
< 50% of clients seeking nature/ ecotourism	7	13,750	1,964 (ranges from 100 to 6,500)	16%	2,240	320
Total Respondents	**18**	**35,520**			**24,010**	

Source: Tour Operator Survey, 2001

1. The table represents the results of the 18 firms who responded to two questions: number of clients served, and number of nature/ecotourism clients.

There were 10 additional firms who chose not to give precise numbers in their responses. However, if we use the averages provided in Table 3.3, and extrapolate to the other 10 firms, we can say that:

40% of companies responding (4) have > 50% of clients seeking nature/ ecotourism		
• thus if we assume 4 of the 10 remaining companies fall into this category	4 x 1,979	= 7,916
60% of companies (6) have <50% of clients seeking nature/ ecotourism		
• thus if we assume 6 of the10 companies fall into this category	6 x 320	= 1,920
One additional firm has 500 ecotourists		500
Thus the number of nature/ecotourists in the remaining firms is:	**7,916 + 1,920 + 500**	**= 10,336**

> • **Therefore, together with those ecotourists in the table above, the total number of nature/ecotourists handled per year by the 29 tour operators surveyed is around 30,000**

While this approximates the total number of outbound ecotourists handled by Canadian tour operators, this is an approximation only, because: some operators handle both domestic and outbound travel; also it is possible that other operators may handle outbound ecotourists, but did not reply to the survey. While these numbers are not precisely known, the figure provided is a good approximation of Canadian outbound nature/ecotourists who use the services of tour operators. There are, of course, many more Canadian ecotourists who use the services of tour operators for travel within Canada, however inbound and domestic tour operators were not the focus of this study. Estimate of Canadian Nature Tourists.

Statistics Canada conducted special runs of their visitors for this study, focusing on those who visit parks and historic sites. The results provide approximate percentages and numbers of those likely to be interested in nature tourism (rather than in ecotourism). The following results emerge:

Population interested in national or other parks or historic sites	
(total of independent and tour groups)*	**Trips**
Canadian visits to parks in Canada (10%)	4.4 million
Canadian visits to parks in the US (20%)	8.5 million
Canadian visits to parks internationally (40%)	**1.8 million**

* Note the US and international figures are the same as in Figure 3.1

> • **2000 Total FIT trips to parks in Canada, US and Internationally**   **14.7 million**

3.3 Ecotourism Markets: Socio-Demographic Characteristics

The information on ecotourism markets is gleaned from a number of studies in Canada, as well as special data runs of two surveys. Appendix E details the key findings of all the available surveys of Canadians. The core information in the following sections comes from the 2001 Tour Operator Survey, and the special data runs of the Canadians interested in nature, adventure and culture, surveyed in 1994, and selected by "purer" ecotourist category (referred to below as "Canadian Ecotourists"). These were conducted specially for this study. The following section summarises the key points of ecotourists' socio-demographic characteristics.

Origins

- **Almost half (48%) of visitors to national parks internationally, were from Ontario** (Statistics Canada 2001. This is reasonable since it reflects the fact that Ontario residents represent about half the international travel in any activity category. Ontario is followed by BC (18%) and Quebec (17%).

- **The tour operator clients come from several areas of Canada. If the operator was based in one region, it followed that that region usually provided core markets.** Approximately 1/3 of operators' clients were from Ontario, 1/3 from the East, and 1/3 from the West/Northern Canada.

Household Income

What is remarkable is the high proportion of households in the over $70,000 income bracket – it ranges from 19% to 37%, depending on which survey is reviewed.

- **All the surveys show a very high household income.**

Age

In all of the surveys, ages range tremendously, but most surveys show a concentration in mid to older age groups, particularly 40 to 65 year olds. The Canadian independent ecotourist survey, however, tends to reveal an emphasis on slightly younger markets, although there are still 25% of markets over age 55 (see Figure 3.2).

Figure 3.2: Canadian Independent Ecotourists: Age

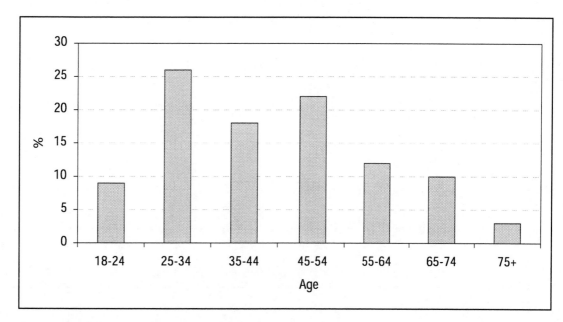

Source: Special Canadian Ecotourist Runs of 1994 survey

- **Independent ecotourists tend to be concentrated in the age ranges 25-54**

- **Surveys found 23% - 45% of independent ecotourists are over age 55**

The ecotourism focus group responses also indicated that travel party ages ranges widely (from children to 75 years of age, with the 40s predominating).

Tour operators attract clients of various ages (Figure 3.3). Ages will vary with a number of factors, particularly the product type offered. Most operators handled about 4 or 5 age groups, and their markets ranged across all ages. However, as both the average percentages of markets, as well as the number of operators dealing with each age range shows, **the middle and older ages are the core markets (aged 45-64), and 53% of operators' products attract this age range**. In addition, it should be noted that the senior markets (65-74) are also quite substantial (16%). Only 4 operators indicated their nature/ecotourism markets were in every age range – in other words, package products tend to attract a specific age range niche.

Figure 3.3:   **_Tour Operator Ecotourist Markets: Age Ranges_**

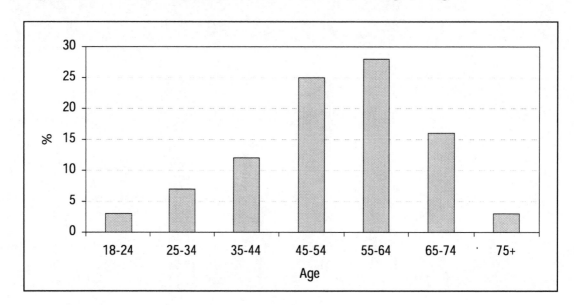

Source: Tour Operator Survey, 2001

- **Tour operators attract older ecotourists, with 55-64 being the main age range**

- **It appears that independent ecotourists are in somewhat younger age brackets, while tour operators tend to attract older markets**

Gender

In the only survey results where males dominate (the Ontario mail-back survey) this is likely related to the fact the activities focussed on adventure. In the other surveys, either the proportions are approximately equal, or females dominate slightly.

- **There are approximately equal numbers of males and females recorded in the various surveys of independent tourists**

For tour operators, females were a higher percentage of their eco/nature tourism markets (56%), over males (44%). The highest proportion of females for any one operator was 70%, Only two operators had a greater percentage of males (55% and 80%) and both operators had "adventure" in their name and in their focus. **All operators dealt with both men and women.**

- **Tour operators had slightly more females than males**

Household Composition

There is generally little information on household composition. The special runs of Canadian Ecotourists indicates that 44% are couples, 38% are couples with children, and 14% travel alone (Figure 3.4).

- **44% of ecotourists are couples; 38% are couples with children**

Figure 3.4: Canadian Ecotourist Household Composition

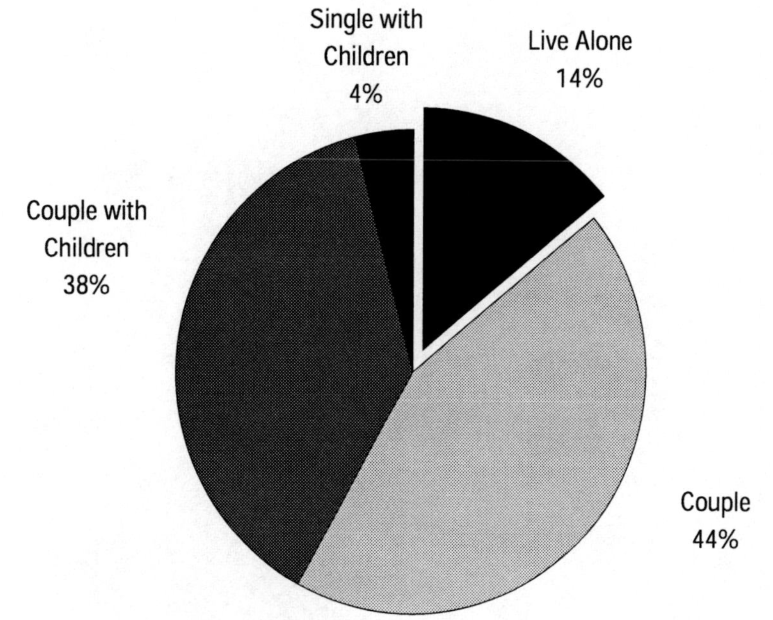

Source: Special Canadian Ecotourist data runs of 1994 survey

Education

Canadian ecotourists are a very highly educated group of people (Figure 3.5). For example, the numbers who have completed college range from 24% to 65%, depending on the specific survey.

- **Canadian ecotourists are a very highly educated group**

Figure 3.5: Canadian Ecotourist Education Level

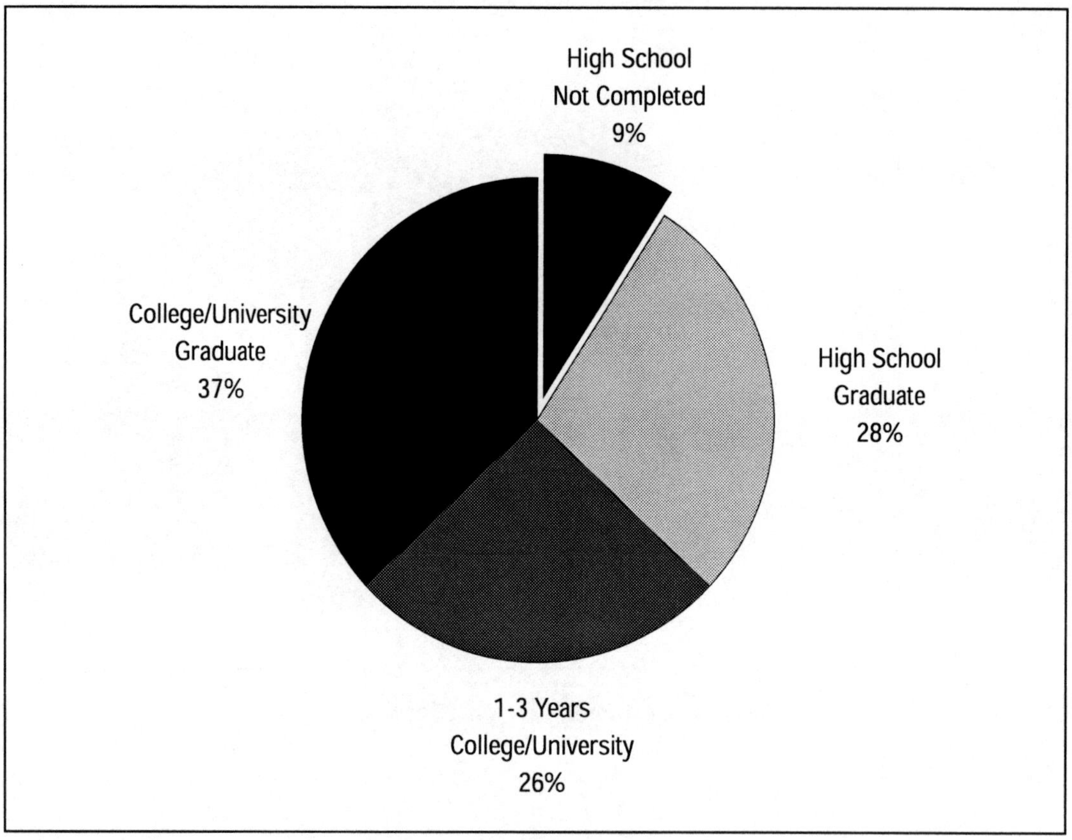

High School
Not Completed
9%

College/University
Graduate
37%

High School
Graduate
28%

1-3 Years
College/University
26%

Source: Special Canadian Ecotourist data runs of 1994 survey

Party Composition/ Travelling Companions

Couples were the predominant party composition for Canadian ecotourists (52%), whether from one household or more than one household (30% + 22%). In addition, families were significant, at 35% (Figure 3.6). This is relatively similar to the Statistics Canada (2000) survey of returning Canadians who had visited parks (50% were couples), and indeed the average party size was similar – 1.95 people.

Figure 3.6: Party Composition of Canadian Ecotourist Trips

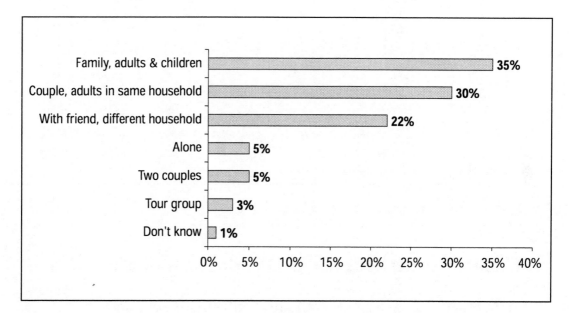

Source: Special Canadian Ecotourist data runs of 1994 survey

The ecotourism focus group indicated the couples and single travellers comprise the bulk of the travel party. When asked how many people they usually travelled with on an ecotourism trip (party size), **the most usual response was in a couple**.

- **Tour operators indicated that single travellers (48%) and couples (45%) represent the bulk of the nature/ecotourism market segments** (Figure 3.7).

Figure 3.7: Tour Operator Travel Parties

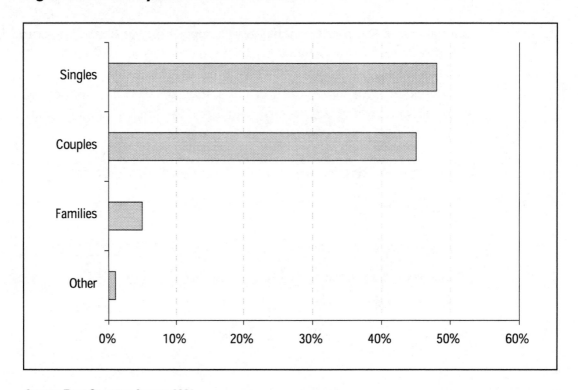

Source: Tour Operator Survey, 2001

3.4   Nature and Ecotourism Product Characteristics

3.4.1 Length of Last Trip: Overall and Ecotourism Portion

The length of trip is a complex element. It is often the case that ecotourists do not necessarily wish to spend their whole trip on an ecotourism vacation. However, it is the length of the total trip, only, that most surveys examine.

- **The Statistics Canada surveys of returning international parks visitors shows that fully a third of respondents were gone for over 17 nights.**

- **The average trip duration was 18.35 nights.**

For the one survey of Canadian ecotourists, which asked about length of total trip, *and* the length of *ecotourism portion*, a different picture emerges (Figure 3.8). The most popular whole trip was over 14 days, followed by 8-14 days. However, the ecotourism portion of the trip was 4-7 days for over one third of respondents (36%). Nevertheless, longer ecotourism trips were more popular than short (e.g., only 7% of the total sample preferred ecotourism trips of 3 days or less. And fully 55% indicated over a week (23% said 8-14 days, and 32% said over 2 weeks).

Figure 3.8: Length of Total Trip and of Ecotourism Portion

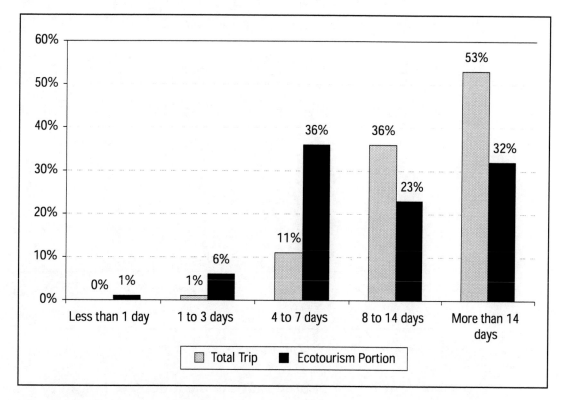

Source: Special Canadian Ecotourist data runs of 1994 survey

- **Ecotourists take longer than average trips, with over half of them taking total trips of over 2 weeks in length.**

- **The ecotourism portion is somewhat less, yet even so, over half these travellers (55%) prefer the ecotourism portion to be over a week.**

Focus group discussions with ecotourists support this. In all cases, the ecotourism trip was shorter than the overall vacation. The total vacation time ranged considerably, with one week, and 3 weeks, being the most common responses. In discussions, the **ecotourism portion of the trip length favoured was identical to the survey findings – 4 to 7 days was the most common response**.

Ecotourism as Stand-Alone Experience, or Part of Classical Vacation?

This question was not specifically asked in any of the major surveys of ecotourists. However, from the previous responses to the Length of Trip Preferences (Figure 3.9), it is clear that ecotourism components are part of another type of vacation for a majority of travellers.

Tour Operator responses supported these findings, with ecotourism trips generally being under a week, whereas the overall trip length was longer.

Figure 3.9: Tour Operator Package Length: Number of Responses

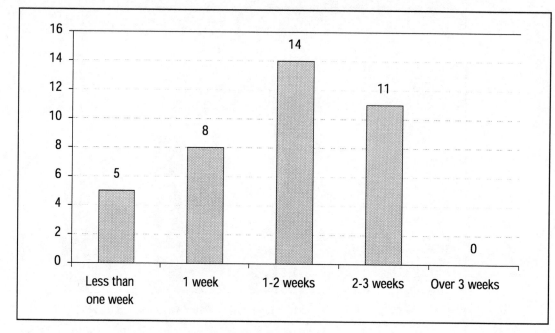

Source: Tour Operator Survey, 2001 (multiple responses)

- **Tour operators indicated that the most popular length of their vacation was 2 weeks**

- **No tour operators offered trips of over 3 weeks.**

3.4.2 Travel Frequency

About a quarter (24%) of Canadian "purer ecotourists" said they took two vacation travel trips outside their Province in the last three years; another quarter (22%) said they took five trips. In all, almost half this group (42%) took more than three trips per year. In the ecotourism focus group, the most common response was one *nature/ecotourism* trip per year.

- **Canadian ecotourists took multiple trips in the year. About half (42%) took more than 3 per year.**

- **As an approximation, about one in three of the international trips mentioned in the ecotourism focus group have a nature/ecotourism component.**

3.4.3 Season/Month Preferred for Travel

The months preferred for travel are overwhelmingly summer (by North American nature tourists), and even more so by the Canadian ecotourist group (Figure 3.10). Nevertheless, shoulder seasons are of significant interest, as are December and January. However, November, February, March and April are challenging months.

Figure 3.10: Canadian Ecotourist Travel Month Preferences

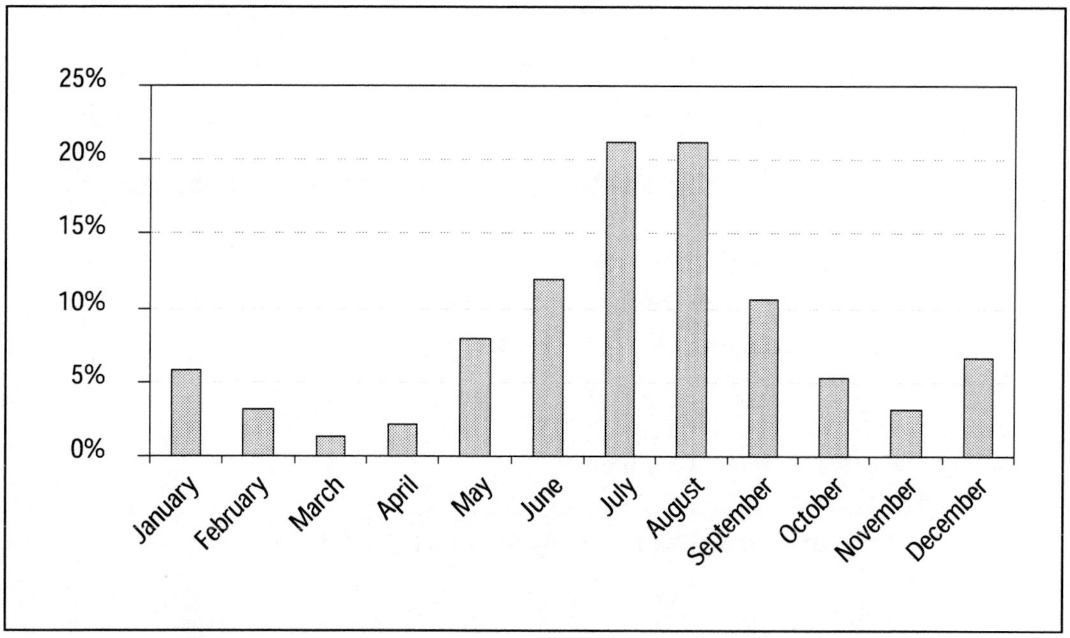

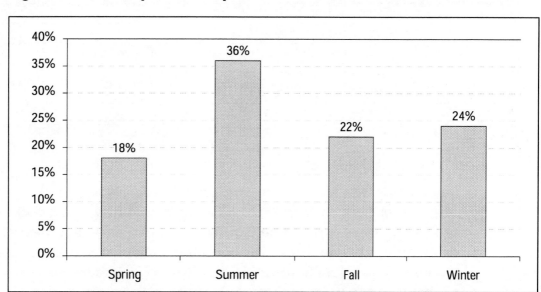

Source: Special Canadian Ecotourist data runs of 1994 survey

- **Most focus group participants said, "it doesn't matter" which month they travelled.**

Tour operator comments shed interesting light on their operations. Whatever the popularity, there are some operators who offer no summer product, and others who offer no winter product. Figure 3.11 shows the number of tour operator responses to preferred season of travel.

Figure 3.11: Tour Operator Responses: Preferred Client Season of Travel

Source: Tour Operator Survey, 2001

- **Tour operators indicated that summer was the most popular season for over one third of their clients.**

- **Spring is the season when tour operators have least packages.**

3.4.5 Commitment to the Destination: Conservation/Local Community Support

Information about conservation or community support activities is very scarce. The main sources are the research conducted specifically for this project – the ecotourist focus group and the tour operator surveys and focus groups.

Tour Operators and their Clients

Tour Operator Destination Support Activities

When provided with a series of possible activities, which support the destination, tour operators responded that their most common activity is hiring locally, followed by partnering locally. These activities appear to not only benefit the destination, but to benefit tour operators' own products. Less attention was paid to conservation/green activities, and other measures.

Types of Activities Operators Support at the Destination, Ranked (N=29)	No. of Responses
• Priority given to hiring locally owned/managed operations (guides, accommodation, etc.)	24
• Partner with local operators (receptive operators, lodges, transportation, etc.)	22
• Environmental conservation (through recycling, waste management, conservation of water and energy, etc.)	17
• Supporting local development projects (environmental or community)	15
• Partner with protected areas	12
• Support scientific/ research programs	12
• Support: CERF – coastal Ecosystems Research Foundation on BC	
VAST – Voluntary Artists Program in Bhutan	
WWF – World Wildlife Fund	
Partner with local NGOs	1

TO Survey, 2001

Despite their wide range of interests and educational level (in which nature-based tourism is but one component), the **clients apparently don't seek ecotourism programs, because they don't know they exist, or what makes them "eco", or why they are important. The operators believe that many more travellers would be interested in ecotourism, if the choices were made better known to them, and they were competitively priced.**

Example: One operator provided the information that they have seen very positive results after taking a trip into an area:

"hoteliers, farmers, hospitals, etc. will say that clients have kept in touch and have kept their promises or further contributed to their cause. Some clients come back year after year on the same trip because they felt connected to the people through our programs. They get a very warm reception from the local people who appreciate the fact that their country is a desirable destination".

- **Most tour operators said they gave priority to hiring locally, usually for guides**

- **Most tour operators partnered with local operators, such as for accommodation or transportation**

- **More than half the tour operators supported environmental conservation and local development projects**

The Web/brochure analysis reveals that while local guides is common for all operators, there are much fewer who provide other examples of local community benefits – only 17 of 29 operators mention other benefits. When it came to conservation activities, less than a third (8 of 29) really have any kind of specific conservation focus or demonstrate understanding.

With respect to conservation, of the 14 operators that address this, 7 seem to be taking substantial action, with program activities such as:

- Ecotourism Standards Program for Tour Operators with NGOs
- Creation of a Charter for all Travellers
- Wildlife Viewing Guidelines
- ECOFUND created
- Creation of guidelines: The Environment and Our Commitment to You
- Protocol on Environment Protection to the Antarctic
- Conservation Fund created by the operator

With respect to group size, only half the operators mention this at all). Four of these merely say "small" groups. However, the meaning of small ranges from 2 to 50, with the commonest being fewer than 15 people.

- **25% of the operators in the Web/brochure analysis indicated group sizes of <15 people**

- **1/3 of operators demonstrate understanding of conservation, and 1/4 are taking substantial action**

- **Very few operators say they donate money to conservation in the Web/brochure materials**

Tour Operators Views on Encouraging Client Donations to the Destination

Operators were split 50:50 in terms of encouraging their clients to make donations at the destination, to conservation, local development, or community projects. Of the ones who did, only one third found that clients reacted favourably to their suggestion.

- **Half the tour operators encouraged clients to donate at the destination**

- **One third of these found clients responded favourably to this suggestion**

Tour Operator Perception of *Client* Involvement in Conservation

Operators were asked the degree of involvement they thought their eco/nature tourism clients had in conservation. Some operators had direct knowledge of client activities, because they themselves are environmental or similar Not For Profits (NFPs). For example, one tour operator is in the process of launching a Volunteer Abroad Program, which may involve Nepal trail clean-ups, etc. Another operator is already engaged in such voluntary conservation/tourism programs, and has Working for Wilderness volunteers, who pay a small fee for the vacation experience, and in addition, work to complete vital conservation projects in partnership with local conservation groups and protected areas managers.

- **About 2/3 of operators (18) said some of their clients contributed to a nature conservation or protection project, by giving money, etc.**

- **About 1/3 of operators said some of their clients participated in a *vacation where they donate their time* or knowledge or skills to a project.**

Independent Ecotourists

The focus group held with (13) ecotourists is the only source of information available for Canadian independent markets on commitment to the destination. Nevertheless, it provides good indicative information, which is summarised below.

Views on Tour Operator Support for the Destination

- **Half the ecotourists in the focus group felt it was very/important for operators to benefit the destination (e.g., local people, the environment, local culture)**

When asked what their tour operator *actually did* on a previous trip, over one third mentioned specific activities (e.g., use of local guides, solar panels, composting; giving priority to hiring locally, partnering with local operators, supporting local development projects, supporting scientific programs; environmental conservation, partnering with protected areas, encouraging clients to support conservation or related causes; sharing profits with locals).

Ecotourists seem to be more concerned that *in the future* their tour operator should be involved in a range of destination support activities. Only a handful of respondents knew from operators' advertising materials about those activities, which benefit the destination. This seems to reveal an opportunity area for responsible tour operators to promote their benefits to the destination.

Views on the Most Important Tour Operator Destination Support Activities

Ecotourists were asked to rank a range of tour operator activities for level of importance. The following activities were supported by over half the ecotourists: Give priority for hiring locally; Environmental Conservation; Supporting local development projects; Support scientific/research programs; Partner with local operators; Partner with protected areas.

- **Independent ecotourists think "hiring locally" is the most important operator activity in the destination**

Views on Client Support for the Destination and for Conservation

- **Not all independent ecotourists would respond positively to operators suggesting they consider contributing to conservation or community support. Most ecotourists would likely ask operators questions before making decisions**

Some ecotourists would be annoyed by or sceptical of tour operator suggestions.

- **The best approach for tour operators suggesting that clients make contributions, is to put such suggestions and information in the first contact point with ecotourists, such as in their brochures**

Ecotourists were asked to rate how important it was that they, personally, (rather than the tour operator) benefit the destination.

- **Almost all the ecotourists (11) felt it was very important for them, personally, to benefit the destination**

- **Approximately half the ecotourists said they currently donate money to benefit charitable or conservation organisations, and contribute to nature conservation projects (not necessarily in the destination)**

Over one third of ecotourists belong to organisations or causes. Further information in an Environment Canada report (2001) found that 1.3 million Canadians aged 15 or over were members of, or contributors to nature-related organisations (e.g., naturalist, conservation or sportsmen's clubs). Over half this number contribute to conservation causes (0.76 million). Ecotourists in the focus group represented a higher than average (Canadian) propensity to belong to nature-related organisations.

In the future, ecotourists would be likely to:

1. Participate in research or scientific expeditions, or research vacations (e.g., science, clean up, voluntary activities which benefit environment/community)

2. Volunteer (e.g., for community/development/conservation projects; or with programs such as Canada World Youth, etc.)

3. Contribute through spending at the destination – food, lodgings, gifts & souvenirs

4. Investigate any trips or tours, to ensure minimal environmental impact, and employment of locals

- ***Overall, some tour operators actively support the destinations, but the most prominent activity (local employment or partnering with local operators) benefits the operators at least as much as the destination. There was less operator support for activities, which did not also benefit their products/packages. About a quarter seem to be taking conservation seriously.***

- ***Overall, independent ecotourists find that taking a tour/vacation which supports the destination is very/important, however, participants tended to place slightly more responsibility on tour operators.***

3.5 Ecotourism Destinations

Destinations Visited by Ecotourists

Canadian ecotourists surveyed in 1994 were asked about the countries they had visited in their last trip. Canada accounted for half the responses, the US accounted for a quarter of the responses, and the other continents were Mexico (8%), Europe (7%), the Caribbean (6%), and South and Central America (3%).

- **Although Canadians were most interested in their own country for their next ecotourism trip, a quarter of Canadian ecotourists (24%) went overseas for their ecotourism trip.**

This wide range of destinations is echoed by the focus group with ecotourists, although the latter group was more evenly spread through destinations. The destinations include:

Canada
US
International (12)

Europe	Scotland, France, Norway, Sweden, Finland, Denmark, Germany, Italy, Bulgaria, Romania, England,
Caribbean	Trinidad & Tobago, US Virgin Islands, Bermuda, interested in Cuba, British Virgin Islands
Asia Pacific	Nepal, Malaysia, Borneo, Thailand, New Zealand
South America	Bolivia, Ecuador, Galapagos, Venezuela, interested in Patagonia
Central America	Mexico, interested in Costa Rica

- **Ecotourists in the focus group had visited a very large range of countries and continents – they are experienced travellers**

Destinations Offered by Tour Operators

Operators surveyed for this project were asked what destinations they sold outside Canada as nature/ecotourism destinations. Canada is a significant ecotourism destination, and there are many other operators who are inbound only. They may well handle Canadians interested in a Canadian ecotourism experience. Thus, the full range of Canadian domestic ecotourism through tour operators is not captured by primary research for this project. Responses (representing the average percentage of nature/ecotourism products sold) were:

Canada	27%
US	12%
International	56%

It should be noted that these findings are averages: a few of the operators sold more than half their product in Canada; some of the operators don't sell any Canadian product; but most operators (62%) sell a large proportion of international product.

- **Well over half the tour operators sell a large (rather than small) proportion of international product**

Of the international destinations mentioned by tour operators, all continents are sold. Many operators did not give countries as destinations, only global regions. The following list illustrates the frequency of the regions mentioned, and many of the countries were mentioned multiple times:

Latin America (17)	Ecuador, Argentina, Brazil, Guyana, Venezuela, Chile, Peru, Galapagos, Amazon, Patagonia, Bolivia, Colombia, Peru
Central America (16)	Costa Rica, Panama, Belize
Asia Pacific (15)	India, China, Tibet, Indonesia, New Zealand, Nepal, New Zealand, Thailand, Australia, Malaysia, Philippines, Borneo, Papua New Guinea
Africa (14)	South Africa, Kenya, Tanzania, Madagascar, Bhutan, Morocco, Namibia, Botswana, Zambia, Egypt, Ethiopia, Zimbabwe
Europe (13)	Iceland, Italy, Ireland, Scotland, England, France, Ireland, Wales, Sweden, Greece, Turkey, Spain, Czech Republic, Switzerland
Caribbean (10)	Honduras, Belize, Bermuda, Cuba, Dominica, St. Vincent & the Grenadines, Barbados, Grenada, Jamaica, Trinidad & Tobago, Turks & Caicos, Antigua
Other (6)	Antarctica, Greenland, High Arctic Canada, Middle East

- **The international products sold by tour operators essentially cover every continent**

- **The main destinations appear to be "exotic", particularly Latin/Central America, Asia, and Africa**

For those operators who sold ecotourism products as 50% or more of their total offerings, the regions/countries most frequently mentioned are: Latin America (especially Ecuador/Galapagos); Central America (especially Costa Rica); Asia Pacific; Africa.

3.6 Cost and Pricing

Independent Travellers' Willingness to Pay

The willingness to pay for independent travellers surveyed is shown on Figure 3.12. These vary dramatically. It has been suggested that the target populations for survey may determine willingness to pay. For example, some results are based on surveys of Canadians going to such destinations as Kenya, or Costa Rica, etc. The average expenditure of these respondents will be higher than surveys of ecotourists in general. At the opposite end is Statistics Canada's survey of returning Canadians who have visited a park internationally (these could be described as general nature tourists). There, a third of respondents have spent less than $2,000, and only 19% paid over $6,000.

Random surveys (rather than those targeting populations travelling to exotic destinations) are likely to give results more appropriately representing the average ecotourist, as in the special runs conducted for this study. It found that the willingness to pay of the Canadian ecotourists is lower than might have been expected (certainly lower than their US counterparts). High-end spenders are lower, with only 11% are willing to pay over $3,000 for the total trip including transportation, while those who are willing to pay up to $3,000 represent the bulk (81%) of respondents. On the other hand, if one views a reasonable package cost for a week, it is not insignificant that over 10% of a target population will pay over $3,000 (and 24% would pay over $2,000 for a one-week package). In addition, it is important to note that these costs are based on 1994 dollars. The inflation factor would increase this amount 7 years later.

- **Over a quarter of Canadian ecotourists (27%) are willing to pay $1,501-$3,000 for an ecotourism trip**

- **11% are willing to pay over $3,000 for an ecotourism trip**

Figure 3.12: Canadian Ecotourist Willingness to Pay

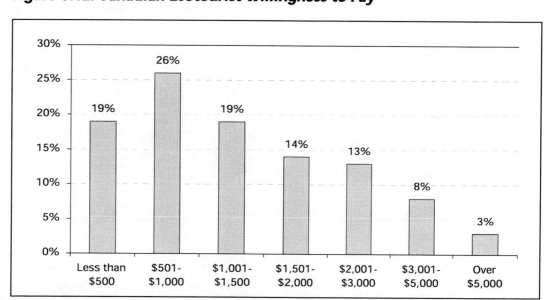

Source: Special Canadian Ecotourist data runs of 1994 survey

The ecotourism focus group also indicated that the lower-end expenditures were usual, with $1,001-$2,000 being the preferred range.

- **Most ecotourist focus group respondents were willing to pay more for packages, which benefited the sustainability of the destination.** It was quite common for respondents to indicate this would be 10% to 15% more than the previous price they had indicated willingness to pay.

Prices of Tour Operator Packages

Canada is 7th in the list of the top tourism spenders in the world (World Tourism Organization, quoted in Travel Industry Publishing Company 2001). Thus, we would expect to see a range of pricing for ecotourism and related experiences.

Canadian eco-adventure operators were surveyed for product prices (Table 3.4). These prices are presented in terms of average price per day, and average number of days.

Table 3.4: Canadian Product Prices, 1995

Product	Average Price Per Day $	Average Number of Days
Nature Observation	172	5.3
Wildlife Viewing		
Bird watching	101	6.5
Polar bear watching	313	5.4
Seal pup watching	4.75/hr	2.5 hr
Other wildlife (bear, moose caribou, bison, etc.)	337.50	7.0
Water adventure products		
Canoeing	87	6.5
Sea kayaking	113	5.7
River kayaking	100	3.6
Rafting	135	4.3
Sailing	171	5.9
Scuba diving	194	4.2
Land adventure products		
Hiking	135	6.1
Rock/ice climbing	113	4.7
Trail riding	100.5	5.0
Bicycling	116	5.6
Winter adventure products		
Dog sledding	193	3
Cross-country skiing	110	4.5
Snowmobiling	179	4.1
Other winter (toboggan, snow-shoeing, heli-skiing)	464	5.7
Air adventure (hot air ballooning)	92.50/hr	2.5 hr
Other (e.g., native culture, jet skiing, motorcycling)	383	X

Source: Tourism Canada 1995

Average daily prices of activities in 1995 ranged from highs of over $464 for specific winter activities, or over $313 for polar bear watching, to lows of $87 for canoeing, and seal pup watching was incredibly low, at less than $5 per hour. These prices may have increased over the intervening years.

Tour operators were asked in the 2001 survey and focus groups, about the average cost, per person, for a one-week nature/ecotourism package (Figure 3.13). The most frequent responses were in the $2,000 - $3,00 range, followed closely by $1,500-$2,000 packages and $3,001-$5,000 packages. This is supported by the Web/brochure analysis.

Figure 3.13: Average Cost of One-Week Package: Percentage of Responses

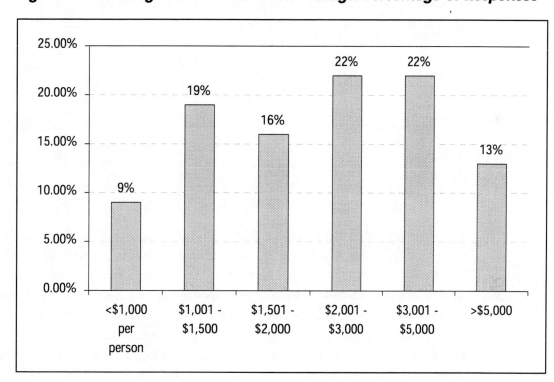

Source: Tour Operator Survey, 2001

- **Almost a quarter of tour operators said the $2,001-$3,000 packages were most popular**

- **Almost a quarter of tour operators said the $3,001-$5,000 packages were most popular**

3.7 Past and Expected Future Trends

Growth in Nature Tourism and Ecotourism

Tour operators surveyed for this project indicated that the trends over the last few years have generally been very positive with respect to both the total number of clients, and with respect to nature/ecotourism clients.

- **All but two operators had seen a growth in total tourism products.**

Av. Growth in nature/ecotourism p.a. over last 3 years (25 operators)	
Decline in Clients	**(1)**
Staying the Same	**(2)**
"growing"	(6)
0-5%	(2)
6-10%	(3)
11-19%	(1)
20-34%	(5)
35-49%	(1)
50-74%	(4)
75-100%	–

Only one operator indicated a decline in *nature/ecotourism* markets. This was a Not-for-Profit (NFP), which experienced a decline in both total number of clients and in nature/ecotourism clients). This is of interest, because in the research for this project, and in contacting other NFPs, it was discovered that certain NFPs which for many years had successfully organised international nature/ecotourism types of trips (e.g., zoos or universities, museums), have stopped organising such trips, because their clientele were declining overall; they suggest this is because of the numbers of commercial tour operators who have sprung up to focus on this nature/ecotourism market niche. Two other operators said the number of clients was staying the same (which is not necessarily a bad thing).

All other operators (22) indicated that *nature/ecotourism* clients are growing, and that overall business is growing. The findings of those who provided specific information are presented below.

The average growth rate presented by operators were:

- **A growth rate of 29% for nature and ecotourism clients of tour operators was experienced (of the 22 operators who said their business was growing)**

Tour operators were asked about their expectations for the future. All but two were optimistic of growth in their nature/ecotourism markets (Table 3.5).

Table 3.5: Tour Operators' Future Expectations of Market Growth

Expected Future	In Operator's Markets, Overall	In Operator's Nature/Ecotourism Markets
Declining	1	1
Staying the Same	2	1
Growing	24	25
Total Respondents	**27**	**27**

Source: Tour Operator Survey, 2001

If one assumes that the growth rate for the future is the same as the growth rate of the past 3 years, one could project growth of:

- **up to 35% for *total* product offerings, including those whose nature/ecotourism product is 100% of business**

- **29% for *nature and ecotourism* products**

General Trends Affecting Nature and Ecotourism

In 1994, the North American **travel trade** was surveyed about their nature/adventure/culture products (HLA/ARA 1994, Travel Trade Survey of 120 operators). When asked about emerging market trends related to ecotourism, operators gave a number of emerging trends. These are still relevant, and are described below:

- **Growth of ecotourism (38)**

The major travel trade response was growth in "ecotourism itself" as the major trend. Operators reported enormous growth in this area, with very emphatic comments, such as: "the wave of the future", "booming", "huge growth", really growing, really hot". This is borne out by the 2001 survey of Canadian tour operators conducted for this study, with respect to their recent growth in business, and also in their predictions of growth in future business.

- **Growth of soft adventure (23)**

Many operators anticipated a general increase in soft adventure, with physically active experiences in a natural setting (rather than more sedentary trips). Thus hiking, rafting, cycling, etc. were increasing. This is supported by the trends identified by Tourism Canada (1995) related to a growing demand for open spaces, clean air, forests, rivers, and lakes and outdoor activities in these settings. However, with the major markets being more urban, packages are being developed for those who have no initial skills or information about the activities. These soft adventure activities are being geared to more generalist and less specialist markets. This results in:

- A greater need for amenities
- Higher level of services
- Activities requiring lower levels of specialist skills
- More responsibility and care of the client by the travel trade

- **Increase in environmental concerns (16)**

A number of operators felt that concern for the environment was becoming an increasingly important issue. This involves such elements as:

- Low-impact tourism, with no harm to the environment
- Increasing support for local conservation efforts
- A move from consumptive to non-consumptive activities (e.g. hunting to photography, or fishing to catch-and-release)

- **Growth in popularity of specific outdoor activities (14)**

Those activities specifically mentioned as growing, included hiking, cycling, boating/cruising, kayaking, scuba/watersports and cattle drives. A number of these observations, such as bicycling, are supported by the other studies examined for this project.

- **Increasing interest in educational trips (13)**

The move to educational trips was noted. People want to travel with a goal of learning through:

- Thematic tours (e.g., historical, cultural)
- Educational tours (e.g., history and culture and skills)

This trend is certainly evident in Canada, where learning travel is sometimes being called *Ed-ventures*. This includes a spectrum of interests, ranging from general interest learning while travelling (e.g., guided tours and interpretive programs) to learning travel programs (group or FIT travel) to purposeful learning and travel (e.g., student exchanges or conferences). The most common form is general interest learning while travelling.

- **Aging population and change in ecotourism clientele (11)**

The increase in soft adventure was stated to be more a reflection of the aging population, than an independent trend. As more active people are getting older, they are seeking less strenuous activities. There are implications for ecotourism, in that softer ecotourism opportunities will be demanded.

- **Other trends (8)**

    Tour operators also noted other trends:

    - Increase in families travelling together
    - Emphasis on value for money
    - Combination trips – 2 or more activities
    - Increase in number of protected areas
    - Move from group tours to individual itineraries, or at least smaller groups
    - People being willing to endure more hardships for increased wilderness experience
    - Decrease in quality of wilderness
    - Greater competition in the travel trade for ecotourism
    - Shorter trips
    - Increased wildlife viewing

Comments from the 2001 tour operator survey, the tour operator focus groups, and the ecotourist focus groups reinforce the fact that many of these trends have continued throughout the 1990s to 2001.

In addition, other new trends or tendencies mentioned by the tour operators in surveys or focus groups include:

- Recognition (e.g., through awards) of those operators truly doing something for the environment
- Conservation vacations, or volunteer vacations, particularly for younger markets
- Sale of tourist icons is successful (e.g., polar bears, Machupicchu, Galapagos, Everest)
- Incorporation of culture and cultural landscapes is important
- Tour operators adopting or contributing to conservation or similar projects
- The future includes experiences off the beaten track and the "never been done before" adventure
- Small group travel is becoming increasingly important, with clients being attracted because groups are small (considered to be 10-16 people)
- Growth in market use of internet for research and information about companies and destinations
- Themed trips (e.g., around bird watching, Mayan history)

Future Ecotourism Destinations Preferred

In terms of *future visits*, Canada featured as the destination of choice for Canadian ecotourists (70%) even more so than in the past (50%). Interest in the US also declined between last and next trip (24% vs. 10%). This may be because Canada, besides being a strong origin country for international tourists, is a world destination for all types of ecotourists, and there has been a growth in the Canadian industry and destinations offering ecotourism product over the last decade.

The 1994 survey of North Americans asked about last and next trip preferences. The responses of all Canadians were analysed, as well as the "purer" Canadian ecotourist sample. The findings are shown on Figure 3.14. It is interesting to note that the interest in Canadian ecotourism destinations may well vary within the country. For example, the 1994 survey found that 53% of those from Toronto preferred a Canadian destination, while 75% of respondents from Winnipeg desired Canada.

Figure 3.14: Destinations of interest to North American Nature Tourists and Purer Canadian Ecotourists

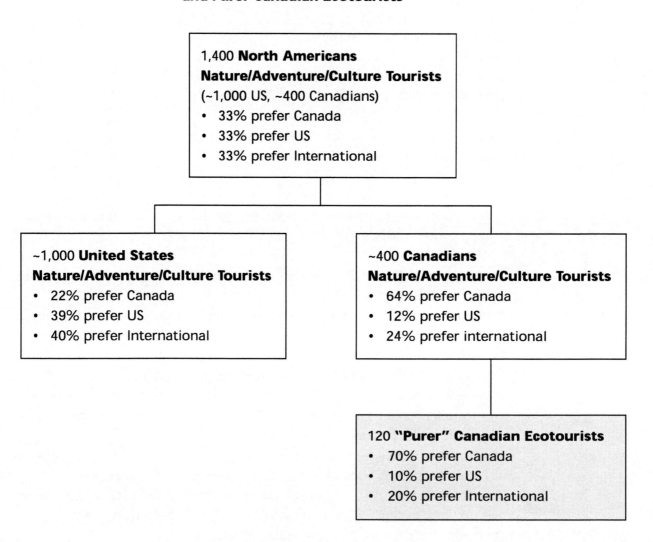

1,400 **North Americans Nature/Adventure/Culture Tourists** (~1,000 US, ~400 Canadians)
- 33% prefer Canada
- 33% prefer US
- 33% prefer International

~1,000 **United States Nature/Adventure/Culture Tourists**
- 22% prefer Canada
- 39% prefer US
- 40% prefer International

~400 **Canadians Nature/Adventure/Culture Tourists**
- 64% prefer Canada
- 12% prefer US
- 24% prefer international

120 **"Purer" Canadian Ecotourists**
- 70% prefer Canada
- 10% prefer US
- 20% prefer International

- **20% of Canadian ecotourists are interested in international destinations on their next trip**

It is significant to see that one fifth of Canadian ecotourists are interested in International destinations, considering there are so many Canadian options in the way of ecotourism.

Focus group participants are also interested in a range of international destinations. These include:

International	
South America	Argentina, Ecuador, Peru, Galapagos, rainforest, Andes, Chile
Central America	Costa Rica
Asia Pacific	Fiji, Bhutan, Mongolia, Central Asia, Laos, Cambodia, Vietnam, N. Thailand, Nepal
Africa	Africa, Morocco, Egypt
Europe	Ireland, Turkey, Germany
Caribbean	Dominican Republic, Cuba
Other	Falkland Islands

- **For their next ecotourism trip, focus group participants mentioned countries in almost every continent except the CIS Countries**

3.8 Conclusions

- Between 18% and 24% of Canadians over 15 are interested in domestic ecotourism-related activities (~5 million)

- In Canada, some outbound tour operators specialise in nature/ecotourism, whereas for others, nature/ecotourism represents only a small part of their total business

- The more a company focuses on nature/ecotourism, the smaller the average number of clients/firm/year is likely to be

- The total number of Canadian nature/ecotourists handled per year by the companies surveyed is over 30,000

- Those interested in visiting parks is used as a proxy for those interested in nature-based tourism. This amounts to 10% of domestic tourist trips (4.4 million), 20% of US tourist trips (8.5 million) and 40% of international tourist trips (1.8 million). International visits to parks has increased steadily (doubled) over the last 15 years

- The household income of ecotourists is relatively high, particularly in the over $70,000 bracket

- The age of independent ecotourists tends to be 25 to 54, while the age of group ecotourists tends to be 45 to74

- There are approximately equal number of males and females involved in nature/ecotourism

- The household composition of ecotourists is mainly couples (44%) and a couple with children (38%)

- Canadian ecotourists are very highly educated, with 2/3 having some college training

- The party composition of ecotourists is mainly family with children, then couples, whereas tour groups are mainly singles, then couples

- The ecotourists trip length (2 weeks and over) is shorter than the overall trip length (over 2 weeks), whereas for tour operators, the most popular package length was 2 weeks

- Ecotourists take multiple trips per year, and 1 in 3 international trips is likely to involve ecotourism

- The summer months are preferred for travel

- There is some commitment to conservation and community support by tour operators, who give priority to hiring locally, usually for guides, as well as some local partnerships and support programs. Half the tour operators encourage their clients to donate to projects at the destination

- The destinations offered by tour operators cover virtually all continents except the CIS Countries, with the main destinations being more exotic – Latin/Central America, Asia, and Africa. 20% of ecotourists are interested in international destinations for their next ecotourism trip

- Over a quarter of Canadian ecotourists would pay $1,500-$3,000 for a week's ecotourism trip, while 11% would pay over $3,000 for such a trip. Many ecotourists are willing to pay more for packages benefiting the destination. The most popular tour packages are priced about $2,000-$5,000 (44%)

- Most tour operators (22) have seen growth (29%) in their tourism and ecotourism products, and expect to see more growth in the future

- Important trends include: increase in ecotourism, increase education travel, growth in soft adventure, concerns about the environment, awards/recognition for environmental activities, conservation vacations, more small group travel, and increasing interest in culture with environment

4. Market Needs, Motivation and Behaviour

4.1 Reasons for Vacation and Destination Attributes

Ecotourism focus group participants had many different reasons for selecting their destination or reason for trip, which echo the results of the survey of Canadian ecotourists. The most frequent response was visiting family and friends. Other reasons were focussed around the activity opportunities. Viewing wildlife was mentioned, but not much as a main reason, as was viewing unusual landscapes. Other reasons focus group participants mentioned were:

- Conservation
- To understand the culture
- Holiday
- Personal interests
- Climate (warm)
- Not many people
- Liberal camping laws
- Proximity to other attractive destination
- Travel writing in foreign destinations
- Easy, fun, road trip
- Unique attraction (e.g., Midnight sun)
- Language
- Opportunity to experience first hand, with top-rated leaders, the various aspects of habitat & species

The 1994 survey of Canadian ecotourists shows important motivational information related to both the last trip and the next ecotourism trip. This provides a dynamic quality to the information (Figures 4.1 and 4.2).

The main reasons for selecting the last vacation trip were: rest, visiting family, and enjoying scenery. However, it is illuminating to compare last trip results with the next trip preferences, these reasons relate first to enjoying scenery, followed by new experiences, then repeating a visit to an enjoyable destination (Figures 3.1 and 4.2.). Scenery is a common element, however, inasmuch as most ecotourism trips are likely to revolve around scenery, some of the other variables are more insightful.

Of significance is the "newness" of the destination/experience. While this is 4th in importance in the last trip (15%), it is second in importance in the next trip (29%), showing that **Canadians are becoming more adventurous in experiences** (and this may also echo the comments of one tour operator who talked about "collectable" or "trophy" destinations).

At the same time, the importance of a known destination should not be discounted. "Been there, want to go again" ranks 5th for the last trip (12%), but for the next trip, it ranks 3rd (20%). This is particularly important for destinations to be aware of – they **need to fulfil market expectations**. In addition, when one considers that word of mouth is the most means that markets use to gain information, it becomes even more **important for destinations and tour operators to satisfy current market expectations**.

Another difference is that while **the most important reason for the *last* trip is rest and relaxation, this is not mentioned at all for the *future* trip**. The purer ecotourists have a large rest component, as well as a family-oriented component.

Figure 4.1: Reasons for Taking the Last Nature/Ecotourism Trip

Reason	Percentage
Rest	31%
Visit family	31%
Enjoy scenery	17%
New experiences	15%
Been there, again	12%
Land activities	9%
See mountains	7%
View wildlife	6%
Culture attractions	4%
Water activities	4%
Study culture	3%
Weather	3%
Business	3%
Less expensive	2%
Visit ocean	1%
Other	6%

Source: Special Canadian Ecotourist data runs of 1994 survey

Figure 4.2: Reasons for Taking the Next Nature/Ecotourism Trip

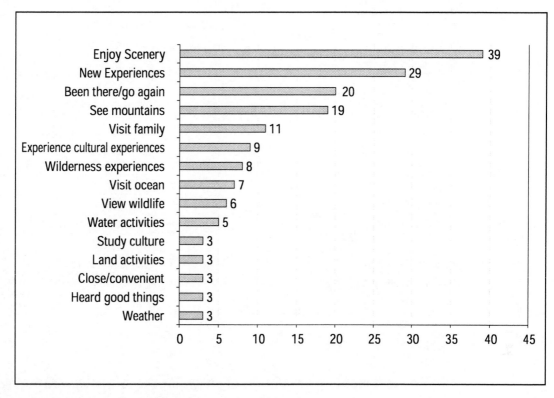

Source: Special Canadian Ecotourist data runs of 1994 survey

4.2 Activity Preferences

Independent Travellers

Appendix E lists all the activities sought by Canadian ecotourists from numerous surveys. The activity preferences for both past and present trips are indicated where possible, to give an idea of the dynamic quality (trends) of market preferences.

However, all of the popular activities are very compatible with a park type of experience – wildlife viewing, hiking, day trips, and water based activities. The special runs of the Statistics Canada (2001) survey of international visitors to parks found that *more general* tourism activities were popular – sightseeing (95%) and shopping (89%) being most popular. Unfortunately, Statistics Canada does not desegregate the activities of respondents who specified "other activity" in the survey. Thus, the other activities associated with visiting parks are not known.

However, the purer Canadian ecotourist survey (120) indicated that hiking and walking were very popular, for both the last trip and even more so for the next trip. Camping was considered an activity by many respondents, and was second highest on the popularity list (30%). In addition, touring was important, and water based activities or sports. The preferred activities by Canadian ecotourists are listed, and arrows are drawn to bolded activities, which have increased significantly in popularity:

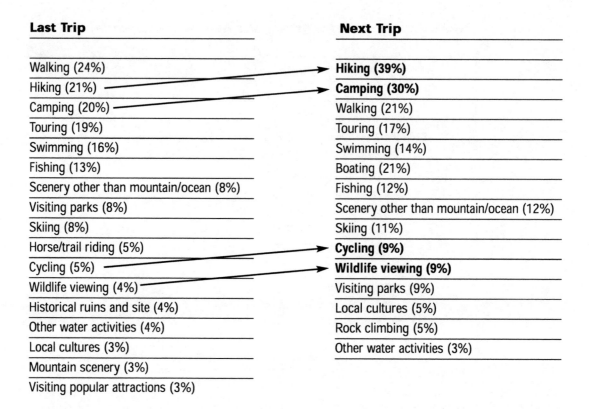

Last Trip	Next Trip
Walking (24%)	**Hiking (39%)**
Hiking (21%)	**Camping (30%)**
Camping (20%)	Walking (21%)
Touring (19%)	Touring (17%)
Swimming (16%)	Swimming (14%)
Fishing (13%)	Boating (21%)
Scenery other than mountain/ocean (8%)	Fishing (12%)
Visiting parks (8%)	Scenery other than mountain/ocean (12%)
Skiing (8%)	Skiing (11%)
Horse/trail riding (5%)	**Cycling (9%)**
Cycling (5%)	**Wildlife viewing (9%)**
Wildlife viewing (4%)	Visiting parks (9%)
Historical ruins and site (4%)	Local cultures (5%)
Other water activities (4%)	Rock climbing (5%)
Local cultures (3%)	Other water activities (3%)
Mountain scenery (3%)	
Visiting popular attractions (3%)	

- **Hiking and walking are extremely high on ecotourists preferred activity lists**

The ecotourist focus group essentially reinforced the findings above. Hiking is a top priority for virtually all the ecotourists, followed by a range of water activities for over half of them (canoeing, kayaking, rafting, and sailing), then by cycling. Also, a recent survey (Lang 2001) shows that hiking or backpacking in wilderness settings are outdoor activities sought more often by all Canadians who took a trip in the last two years (29%), and are likely to be sought by 27% in the next two years.

Tour Operator Clients

The activities sought by tour operators' clients are reflected in the package offerings

These findings are supplemented by a survey of the travel trade where respondents were asked to describe their three most popular ecotourism packages (HLA/ARA 1994, Travel Trade Survey of operators). Canadian tour operators were separated out in this analysis (16 companies). The popular packages were:

Water Based Activities	Land Based Activities	Other Speciality Activities
Canoeing	Hiking/walking	Flying
Rafting	Small bus/van tour	Wildlife Viewing
Boat/Cruise/Sailing	Cycling	Photography
Kayaking	Horseback/ranch	Cultural
Fishing	Mountaineering	
Scuba/snorkelling		

- **The most popular activity tour operator packages include: hiking/walking, bus touring, rafting, boat/cruise/sailing, wildlife viewing, cycling, canoeing and kayaking.**

The Web/brochure analysis reflects the range of activities independent ecotourists are seeking. In addition, they place a high importance on hiking and walking, and a high focus on a range of cultural experiences and interactions.

4.3 Accommodation Sought

Independent Travellers

Appendix E compares the accommodation preferences of nature/ecotourists according to different surveys. Statistics Canada's survey of returning international Canadians who visited parks indicates over half the nature tourists in 2000 (56%) stayed in hotels/motels. Similarly, the Canadian ecotourists (1994) were most interested in hotels/motels for both their previous and next trips (Figures 4.3 shows their next trip preference). It should be noted that the relatively high preference for conventional accommodation might be related to a number of factors, including: respondent lack of familiarity with alternative "adventure accommodation"; available range of accommodation at the destination; a preference to stay in "safe" accommodation in those destinations with greater uncertainties.

Ecotourists provided multiple accommodation responses, indicating a degree of flexibility. This is borne out by the 24% of respondents who had stayed in a combination of types of accommodation on their last such vacation.

- **The largest portion of Canadian ecotourists is interested in conventional hotel/motel accommodation.**

- **However, a significant portion is more interested in accommodation related to the experience itself. For example, 27% are interested in camping in the future.**

- **About half of Canadian ecotourists prefer a midrange level of luxury (52%).**

- **In future, Canadian ecotourists are more interested in basic budget accommodation (46%) than the larger sample of Canadian nature tourists.**

Only 2% of the ecotourists are interested in luxury accommodation.

Figure 4.3: Canadian Ecotourists Accommodation Preferences for their Next Vacation

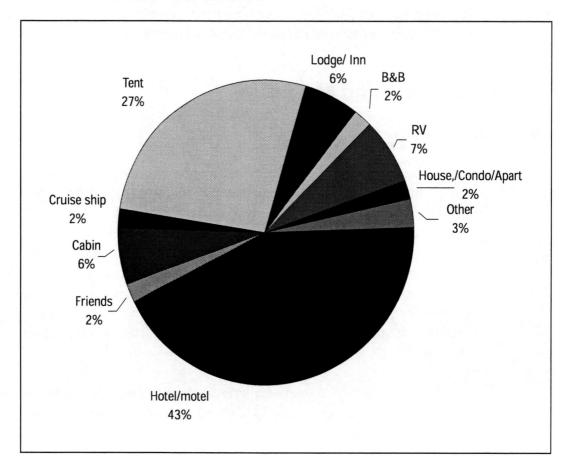

Source: Special Canadian Ecotourist data runs of 1994 survey

The ecotourism focus group reinforced some of these findings. There was less interest in luxury for future accommodation. About half were interested in normal hotel/inn/lodge accommodation, but a significant number (also about half) were **interested in accommodation related to the experience** – for example tents, self-catering cabins, or bed and breakfasts. Also, multiple responses were common, indicating a degree of flexibility. Comments ecotourists in the focus group made about accommodation include:

• should be decent quality, even if rustic
• clean and comfortable
• lodging with private sleeping rooms, private washrooms, dining & bar service
• lodging that practices good environmental management throughout
• smaller accommodations
• professional operation of the facility are important

World Tourism Organization

Tour Operator Clients

Operators were asked to indicate the rough percentage of their business that used the various types of accommodation and levels of luxury, for their nature/ecotourism products. These results are found in Figure 4.4. It should be noted that these are averaged according to totalling operators responses, and don't necessarily represent the total volume of business of operators, aggregated.

Some operators commented that certain lodges are very expensive, but not necessarily very luxurious, thus it was difficult for them to indicate their preference (which is for less expensive lodges – this echoes comments in the ecotourist focus group). Another indicated that one of the biggest issues for them, in accommodation, was cleanliness, as well as having all facilities in working order. The ecotourist focus group also supported this need for cleanliness.

Figure 4.4: Preferred Accommodation for Tour Operator Clients

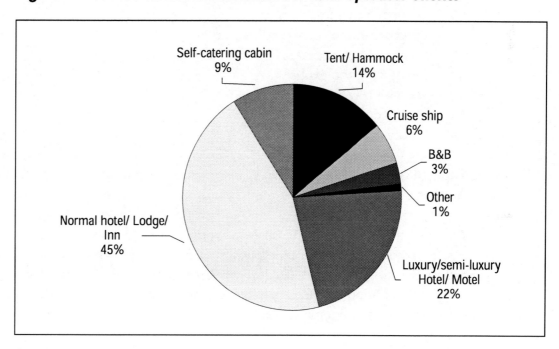

Source: Tour Operator Survey, 2001

4.4 Experiences Sought and Destination Attributes

Independent Ecotourists Ratings

The ecotourist focus group participants rated the importance of the destination attributes for them. The two most important features desired equally by independent travellers are: an interpretative/learning experience and experiencing wilderness and remote areas. These are closely followed by discovering local cultures and foods. Other features, ranked, include:

1. **Experiencing wilderness/remote areas**
2. **Interpretative/learning experience**
3. **Discovering local cultures and foods**
4. Rest and relaxation in natural settings
5. Wildlife viewing
6. Interacting with aboriginal cultures
7. Experiencing parks/protected areas
8. Outdoor activities
9. Contributing to conservation
10. Contributing to local community development
11. Discovering the exotic
12. Socialising with interesting people
13. Knowledgeable guides
14. Luxury accommodation

Luxury accommodation was of very little interest to ecotourists, only getting a weighted average of 1.47 (out of 5), whereas all the other features averaged in the high threes.

Many of the ecotourists in the focus group indicate they are wanting to escape, avoid crowds, and look for quiet, however, they say that **they want rest and relaxation for only a short period of time**. They also indicate their motivations include benefiting the local people in various ways, more so than conservation, although this is also a motivator.

Destination Evaluations

The focus group ecotourists indicated a number of strengths in destinations they had visited. These were also widely ranging, including leaders and guides; quality of landscapes and environment; interactions with the local people including discovering cultures and food; opportunities to contribute to community development; and opportunities to contribute to conservation.

- **Accommodation was mentioned by half the focus group participants as a strength**

- **Locally knowledgeable guides were important as a destination strength**

When asked about the *weaknesses* in the destination, focus group ecotourists gave a range of responses. In addition, participants provided suggestions for what needed to be done about this weakness. Weaknesses included: need for more professional language; having travel arrangements fully in place; ensuring safety of drinking water and living quarters; more modest accommodation. There were few weaknesses discussed.

Tour Operator Ratings

When asked to rate a list of features and attractions as to their level of importance for their clients, operators provided detailed information, shown on Table 4.1 (Tour Operator Survey, 2001). The weighted average for accommodation is slightly higher than it would have been if it had not been for one operator whose clientele is very interested in luxury accommodation.

- **The most important feature desired by clients, according to tour operators, is knowledgeable guides, followed by an interpretative/learning experience, and wildlife viewing opportunities, which have very high ranks**

Table 4.1: Operator Rating of Activities and Features of the Destination Experience

Feature or Attraction	Number of Responses (28 Operators) Importance Rating					
	1	2	3	4	5	Weighted Av.
1. Knowledgeable guides		1	2	7	17	4.48
2. Interpretative/learning experience		2	5	8	12	4.11
3. Wildlife viewing		3	5	7	12	4.04
4. Experiencing wilderness/remote areas	2	2	4	10	9	3.81
5. Outdoor activities	1	3	7	5	11	3.81
6. Discovering the exotic	1	4	6	8	8	3.67
7. Experiencing parks/protected areas	1	4	6	6	8	3.64
8. Discovering local cultures and foods	1	3	6	12	4	3.58
9. Socialising with interesting people	3	1	9	8	8	3.56
10. Interacting with aboriginal cultures	1	6	8	10	3	3.54
11. Contributing to conservation		4	12	8	2	3.31
12. Contributing to local community development	5	8	12	5	2	3.15
13. Rest and relaxation in natural settings	1	10	6	7	2	2.96
14. Luxury accommodation	8	7	5	4	1	2.32
Other (authenticity of & "collectable" experience)					1	

Tour operator survey, 2001

Further comments by tour operators about the most important amenities, services, and strengths required at the destination, to attract them to package product for ecotourists, reinforced some of the messages above (Table 4.2). These open-ended comments may be grouped as follows:

Table 4.2: Tour Operator Suggestions about the Destination

Category	Tour Operator Needs at the Destination
New, Unique or Collectable Location	• Marketability of package desired
	• Chance to visit a new place
	• Highlights that can be packaged as a "collectable experience"
	• Unique and enjoyable destination/outdoor experience/nature product/ viewscape
	• Tourist icons desired (e.g., polar bears, Machu Picchu, Galapagos) to "sell" to clients
Guiding & Interpretation	• Opportunity to leave with knowledge that will result in individual action for conservation
	• Opportunity to learn conservation and natural history skills
	• Professional, knowledgeable subject guides – with university/wilderness education
	• Exceptional, organised, local guides and interpretative service
Wildlife	• Animal species of interest to conservation programs
	• Good opportunities to see animals in their natural habitats
	• Unique and enjoyable wildlife
Habitat/ Environment	• Opportunity to learn more about biology and conservation status of habitat/species
	• Varied habitats/experiences at any one environment
Food	• Good quality food
	• Nutritious and Very varied
Infrastructure	• Reliable and consistent infrastructure
	• Relatively easy access, flight connections
	• Efficient, reliable transportation
Activities & outdoors	• High experiential value
	• Access to nature and outdoor activities
Destination operators & operations	• Good ethical standards of inbound operators
	• Good buying power – well priced, and with good financial stability
	• Willingness to be flexible
	• Genuinely friendly service & staff
	• Chance to interact with local people
	• Locally owned amenities/services & key contact
	• Safety, to limit risk

Tour operator survey, 2001

4.5 Conclusions

- The main reasons for taking a nature/ecotourism trip is scenery. However, of importance to motivations are the desire for new experiences (29%), followed by the knowledge of a place and the desire to return to it (20%).

- The activities most preferred by ecotourists include hiking (39%), camping (30%) and walking (21%).

- The accommodation sought is mainly hotels/motels for both independent eco-tourists and tour groups. However, a significant portion of ecotourists is interested in accommodation, which reflects the ecotourism experience: tents, lodge/inns, and cabins. A portion of tour groups are interested in luxury accommodation, while others are interested in tent/hammocks, and self-catering cabins.

- The most important experiences sought by independent ecotourists are: experiencing wilderness/ remote areas, interpretative/learning experiences, and discovering local cultures and foods. Tour operators said the most important features were knowledgeable guides, interpretative/learning experiences and wildlife viewing.

5. Marketing for Ecotourism in Canada

5.1 Communication Channels

5.1.1 Operators Evaluate Relative Importance of Media Used

Tour operators were asked to indicate the relative importance of the various means they used to reach and communicate with their markets. Figure 5.1 shows the importance rating which operators used. These are established operators, thus a number of media assume that there are pre-existing markets to reach.

Tour operators evaluate word of mouth as the most important way that markets receive information. While it might be considered that tour operators cannot tap into this, in fact, they indicate that the way they best respond to this is to provide an experience, which satisfies or exceeds their current market expectations. One important method is by having excellent quality guides, who are responsible for increasing the number of "repeats" who are in turn responsible for word of mouth promotion. It is also known that companies are beginning to make it easier for customers to communicate about, or recommend their product to others, for example, by making electronic postcards available on their Web sites. This is essentially a form of word of mouth advertising.

Table 5.1: Tour Operator Evaluation of Media for Marketing

Methods to Reach Eco/Nature Tourism Clients	Number of Responses (28 operators)					
	Importance Rating					
	1	2	3	4	5	Weighted Average
Word of mouth		2	3	5	14	4.29
Internet site	1	2	2	10	9	3.70
Specific messages within your general brochures	2	3	4	5	9	3.70
Media releases	1	3	6	6	6	3.59
Target mailings	3	2	5	6	8	3.58
Special eco/ nature brochures	1	3	5	7	3	3.42
Newsletters	4	1	4	7	5	3.38
Advertisements in specialised magazines	1	6	6	6	3	3.18
Travel Agents	4	2	6	4	3	2.85
Trade shows	8	3	6	4	1	2.41

Others presentations; canvas team; continuing education flyers with sponsoring university; in-house catalogue with all programs; associations; FAMs

Source: Tour Operator Survey, 2001

- **Word-of-mouth, the Internet, and messages within their brochure, are felt to be the best communication channels to use. Others are media releases and target mailings**

5.1.2 Types of Information Provided by Tour Operators to Customers

The kinds of information which operators provide their nature/ecotourism clients varies. Those types of information mentioned most frequently include:

- Pre-trip information (26)
- Detailed information about habitats, species, ecosystems visited (22)
- Pre-trip meetings or briefings (20)
- Guidelines for conduct, or codes of ethics for travellers (17)
- Information about cultural traditions, the local context for species protection, conservation programs, NGOs who accept donations for these purposes (16)

Note: One tour operator indicated that often they sell their tours as part of an adult education course where the professor (rather than the tour operator) plays the role of information-provider.

5.1.3 How Ecotourists Get Information about the Destination Ecotourism Opportunities

Tour Operator Media

Previous surveys of ecotourists found that word of mouth was consistently the most important vehicle for obtaining information (Figure 5.1). The Canadian ecotourist survey also found that consulting with travel associations (22%) and travel brochures (16%) and books (15%) were important.

Figure 5.1: Canadian Ecotourist Methods of Obtaining Information

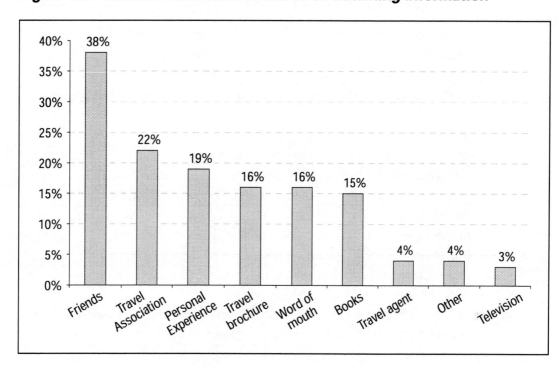

Source: Special Canadian Ecotourist data runs of 1994 survey

- **Friends (38%) are the most important source of information for ecotourists.**

- **Personal experience is also important (19%)**

In effect, "friends, personal experience, and word of mouth (which may include colleagues, neighbours, etc.) are all-important categories of personal contact which are collectively most important to ecotourists, rather than the conventional sources of information which tour operators may more apparently control.

Ecotourists do Research

Typically, ecotourists do a very large amount of research on their selected destination, as the ecotourist focus group discussion revealed. They use maps, atlases, read the local newspapers, scan the internet thoroughly, seek out all literature, get to know the economics of the area, and know most of the options before they go. They ask questions about their potential destinations, and find the more conscientious operators where needed.

Ecotourists said there were a number of media, which influenced their selection of destination. These included: Brochures; Internet; Friends; Travel agents; Print advertising; Radio.

When asked to indicate the specific media that they might use to research their vacation, ecotourists in the focus group make insightful comments (Table 5.2).

Figure 5.2: Canadian Ecotourist Insights into the Media they use

Media Used	Ecotourist Specifics on Media
Word of mouth (10)	• Colleagues, or friends (VIP)
Media releases (9)	• Natural history, educational TV shows, travel TV shows (e.g. Outdoor life network), slides, CBC radio
Advertisements in Specialised Magazines (8)	• American Museum of Natural History; Conservation International; and nature magazines, local paper, Environmental, yoga and health magazines, Outpost; Explore, Outside; and climbing and hiking magazines, National Geographic
Books, Guide and Travel Literature (4)	• Guide books, Lonely Planet, Tour books, book footnotes, and guide books by "average travellers"
Special eco/nature brochures (4)	• Brochures targeting work of school abroad, travel agent, from local destinations, mail request
Internet site (3)	• Internet search, Ron Mader's Ecotourism site, Rough Guide, friend's recommended sites
Target mailings (2)	• From past trips, or requests
Newsletters (2)	• Alpine Club of Canada (BREEZE), Friends
Travel Agents (1)	• Use travel agents for research
Other	• Atlas; Rough Guides; Internal Business; local library; economic journals; encyclopaedias; books;

Ecotourism focus group, 2001

The focus group was asked what attracts them to the media listed above, and where do they look for information. Some relevant comments are the fact that the Web is a core tool for most of them, and the local library is as well. A number browse bookstore shelves, as well as using their friends' books. Most indicate they read and research a great deal, in multiple media. While they read magazines, and want quality information, they don't necessarily want glossy ads and image.

- **Canadian ecotourists are very well educated, and research their destination a great deal, via multiple media**

5.2 Planning and Booking

Planning Lead Time

The amount of time for vacation planning seems to be relatively short. Almost three quarters (72% of Canadian ecotourists make their decisions within 3 months of the vacation. Only 2% planned more than a year ahead. This is supported by the other surveys in Ontario, and for the wider markets of nature and ecotourists in North America.

Booking Method Preference

The ecotourism focus group indicated the most popular method of booking, was for **ecotourists to make arrangements themselves, as they travel (9)**. In addition, these ecotourists, who are known to be strong vacation researchers:

- use the internet, then book direct with the supplier
- use the internet to book
- through club or association
- through travel agent

None mentioned that they currently book through a tour operator; indeed, most indicated that they would *avoid* packages (customised or not) booked at their point of origin in Canada. Focus group participants also indicated that although they would avoid packages, they would consider a package at the destination. Although they prefer to avoid packages now, 11 of the 13 participants had experience some type of packaged travel in the past, but only 3 indicated they would consider a Canadian-based operator in the future.

- **Focus group participants tend to make travel arrangements directly, themselves, and avoid group travel, *unless it is booked at the destination***

5.3 Reaching Ecotourists

Internet

There have been no Canadian studies, which examine the Internet use by ecotourists. However, a recent study (Lang 2001) finds that 37.6% of the Canadian population (18 plus) report using the Internet on a regular basis as a source of information, not just travel information. The use of the Internet as an information source was strongly associated with the frequency with which pleasure trips were taken during the last two years. Thus, 63% of those who had taken 10 or more pleasure trips during the past two year have used the Internet as a source for information, while only 28% of those who did not take a pleasure trip use the Internet regularly.

Also, the use of the Internet as an information source increased sharply with increases in the education level of the respondent and the overall household income, which strongly correspond with the characteristics of ecotourists. Younger respondents were also more likely to use the Internet as an information source, but Internet was quite highly used by affluent mature singles/couples, which are important segments of the ecotourist travel market. These findings are strongly supported by the ecotourism focus group research.

Although 13.3% of North Americans (18 plus) have booked a pleasure trip through the Internet, Canadians (5.2%) were less likely to do this than Americans (14.2%).

- **37.6% of Canadian adults report using the Internet on a regular basis as a source of information, not just travel information**

- **5.2% of Canadians book pleasure trips though the Internet**

- **there is a high correlation between the socio-demographic characteristics of internet users and of Canadian ecotourists**

Memberships

Appendix E details the memberships of nature/ecotourists taken from several surveys. A recent survey (Lang 2001) shows there is a strong positive correlation between the frequency of pleasure travel and likelihood of membership in an organisation – especially memberships in art galleries, museums and nature organizations. The Ontario intercept shows that more belong to environmental organisations (13%) than to outdoor organisations (9%), and this is similar for the Ontario survey – **ecotourists are concerned about the environment**. The Canadian ecotourist survey, also, showed 13% belonging to organisations overall which is somewhat higher than for the overall North American survey from which this sample is drawn. Of those who are members, the most popular clubs or organisations are:

1. Greenpeace
2. National Wildlife Federation
3. Fishing/hunting organisations
4. Other wildlife organisations
5. Outdoor activity club
6. WWF
7. Flower/garden clubs
8. Boy/girl scouts

- **The most popular organisation for Canadian ecotourists to belong to is Greenpeace, followed by outdoor organisations**

We also know that of all Canadians participating in indirect nature-related activities (5.4% - 1.3 million Canadians) are members of or contributors to a nature related organisation, such as naturalist, conservation or sportsmens' clubs (Environment Canada 2001). This means that **ecotourists are more than twice as likely as the general population to belong to clubs or organisations**, particularly those, which are nature-related.

Publications

Appendix E details the publications read by nature/ecotourists. Of North Americans as a whole, almost 2/3 read publications (61%), whereas the Canadian sample of eco-tourists is less likely to read publications (55%). Magazines are the primary print media mentioned, and this is supported by a recent Travel Activities & Motivation Survey, where magazine readership was found to increase as a function of the number of pleasure trips taken over the last few years. This reflects the fact that travel frequency and print media consumption are both positively related to the respondent's education level and household income (Lang 200).

The frequency of travel was especially associated with increases in readership for news magazines, travel magazines and the National Geographic, for Canadians as a whole. Similarly, of those magazines read by Canadian ecotourists, the National Geographic is outstandingly the most popular, for over 1/3 of Canadian ecotourists (39%). Other outdoor, nature based, and hunting and fishing magazines are also of interest to nature-based markets and ecotourists.

National Geographic (39%)   General activity/sports (7%)
Fishing/hunting (9%)   Outdoor Life (4%)
General nature (9%)   Field & Stream (5%)
Canadian Geographic (7%)   Other (Club publications, general travel, wildlife related, Equinox)

- **55% of Canadian ecotourists read publications, of which National Geographic is the most important**

It is also interesting that in the Web/brochure analysis, there was surprisingly little reference to ecotourism by any tour operator. Only 4 of 29 operators mentioned eco-tourism at all. Since 8 operators appeared to be strongly conservation oriented, this might potentially be a missing tool for reaching ecotourists and nature tourists. There is more discussion about operators' perspectives on ecotourism and nature tourism in Appendix A.

5.4 Conclusions

- Tour operators consider that word of mouth is the most important element for marketing their products, followed by the internet, and their brochures

- The types of information the provide to clients includes pre-trip information, environmental details about the destination, and pre-trip briefings

- The main means ecotourists learn about ecotourism destinations is by personal contacts, including: friends, personal experience and word of mouth. All of these shows the importance of personal experience of different types. Ecotourists also do a considerable amount of varied research before their trip. Other sources of information are travel associations, travel brochures, books, specialist magazines and the internet

- Planning lead times are relatively short, and æ of ecotourists decide within 3 months of the vacation

- Independent ecotourists prefer to make travel arrangements themselves, and as they travel

- Ecotourists may be reached by a range of means: the internet (there is a high correlation between ecotourist and internet user characteristics); memberships in organisations (ecotourists are twice as likely as the general public to belong to organisations); and publications (55% of ecotourists read publications, especially National Geographic)

6. Conclusions

- Most ecotourists and tour operators agreed with the WTO definition of ecotourism and nature tourism

- However, although most felt they had a nature and/or ecotourism component in their product offerings, only a handful of operators used the word ecotourism in their marketing materials

- Overall, Canadian markets are growing for international travel

- Continued growth in ecotourism markets is expected, to both domestic and international destinations. The market for nature and adventure is wider and larger

- Tour operators cater to somewhat older markets, and their product offerings are somewhat "softer"

- The quality of environment is very important to Canadians, and ecotourists are concerned about the environment, and conscious about the benefits (or lack of) benefits to the destination

- Core target markets for ecotourists are 45-65 year-olds, with higher education, and above-average income, and women are slightly more prevalent than men, particularly with tour operators

- Although there is interest in the environment, there is also interest in benefiting local peoples, and interaction with them, especially through quality interpretation

- International destinations tend to be relatively wide-ranging and exotic, and tour operators described preferred destinations as being "collectibles". Whereas surveys of Canadian ecotourists revealed a strong interest in Canadian destinations, and 20% interest in international destinations

- The products offered frequently seem to focus on adventure and culture, within natural settings. The international vacations offered average 1-2 weeks, but the ecotourism portion is invariably a part of this more classical vacation

- Canadians are most interested in summer travel, but shoulder seasons have good potential

- 11% of Canadians were willing to pay over $3,000 for an ecotourism trip in 1994 dollars

- Most ecotourists in the focus group were willing to pay more for packages which benefited the sustainability of the destination (environment and local people)

- The activities sought revolve around scenery, and reveal a combination of desire for new experiences, and the desire to go again to a place which satisfied them. Hiking and walking were strong preferences

- Although the largest preference was for conventional hotel/motel accommodation, a range of types is acceptable to Canadian ecotourists, particularly if it reflects the ecotourism experience sought

- The most important destination attributes for operators was: knowledgeable guides, interpretative/learning experiences, and wildlife viewing opportunities

- Friends and word-of-mouth (and personal experience) are the most important information sources

- Independent ecotourists do a tremendous amount of research before a trip (internet & books)

References

Angus Reid Group Inc. 1992. *The Canadian Pleasure travel market Segmentation Study: Outbound Travel Presentation.*

Baxter Publishing. 2000. *Personnel Guide to Canada's Travel Industry.* Baxter Publishing: Toronto.

Canadian Tourism Commission. *Major Markets Overview.* Web publication. **http://www.canadatourism.com/en/ctc/ctx/ctx-ind_watch/tourism_stats/index.cfm**

Clark, W. 1997. Trading Travellers – International Travel Trends. Statistics Canada *Travel-log.* 16(4):1-6. Autumn.

Davis, T. 2001. *Safety, Security Declaration Needed By Canadians.* CTX tourism information exchange, Nov-02, Posted Nov 5.

Eagles and Cascagnette, 1995. Canadian Ecotourists: Who Are They? *Tourism Recreation Research,* V.20 (1):22-28.

Environment Canada. 2001. *The Importance of Nature to Canadians.* **www.ec.gc.ca/nature/**

HLA Consultants and ARA Consulting 1994. *Ecotourism – Nature/Adventure/Culture: Alberta and British Columbia Market Demand Assessment.* 6 Volumes. Canadian Heritage, Industry Canada, BC Ministry of Small Business, tourism and Culture, Alberta Economic Development and Tourism.

Lang Research. 2001. *Travel Activities & Motivation Survey: Overview Report.* **www.tourism.gov.on.ca/english/research/tams.asp**

McDougall, L. 1999. Seniors... A Market to Watch in the next Millennium. Statistics Canada *Travel-log.* 18(4):1-8, Autumn.

Pam Wight & Associates, 1999. *Catalogue of Exemplary Practices in Adventure Travel and Ecotourism.* Canadian Tourism Commission: Ottawa.

Shaienks, D. 2000. The Changing Family and the Evolution of the Canadian Family Travel market, 1980-1998. Statistics Canada *Travel-Log.* 19(2):1-7, Spring.

Statistics Canada: **www.statcan.ca/english/Pgb/People?population/demo10a.htm** 19 Sept. 2001.

Statistics Canada. 1999. *International Travel*, Catalogue no. 66-201.

Statistics Canada 2001. *Canadian Residents* – 2000. Special Data Runs of International Travel Survey.

Statistics Canada and Canadian Tourism Commission. 1999. *Tourism Statistical Digest*, 1999 Edition, based on 1997 data.

Touriscope: International Travel Advance Information. 2000. V 15(12) Statistics Canada Catalogue no. 66-001-PPB V14(12) v16(12)

Tourism Canada. 1995. *Adventure Travel in Canada: An Overview of Product, Market and Business Potential*. Industry Canada, February.

Twynam, G.D., and D.W. Robinson. 1997. *A Market Segmentation Analysis of Desired Ecotourism Opportunities*. Nat. Resource Canada, NODA/NFP Technical Report TR-34. Canadian Forest Service, Great Lakes Forestry Centre: Sault Ste. Marie, Ontario.

Wight, P. 2001. Ecotourists: Not a Homogenous Market Segment, in *The Encyclopaedia of Ecotourism*, D.B. Weaver et al. (eds.) CAB International: Wallingford, UK.

World Tourism Organization 2000. *Proposals of the WTO Relating to Priority Issue Number 9: Clarify the Concepts of Sustainable Tourism and Ecotourism*. Multistakeholder Working Group on Tourism. Madrid. March

Appendix A: Canadian Perspectives on Definitions

Attitudes to the Terms "Nature" and "Ecotourism"

Tour Operators

Tour Operators Agreed with the WTO Definition of Ecotourism

Almost all the operators (26 of 29) agreed with the definition of ecotourism developed by the WTO. It should be noted that the operators were given an opportunity to respond that they completely agreed, didn't really agree, or didn't agree at all. One operator indicated that they would have preferred a "less aggressive" response option, such as simply "agree" (versus "completely agree"). It would be valuable to consider having a broader range of options in future surveys, to obtain the subtleties of the responses. The following chart provides some tour operator comments and perspectives.

Tour Operator Survey (29)	
Don't Agree at All (0)	
Not Really in Agreement (3)	• Don't really agree that ecotourism consists of small groups or individuals • Feels there should be a component added – that of promoting peace through tourism • Believes local economic benefits should be greater, in true ecotourism, through additional fees
Completely Agree (26)	• don't necessarily agree with the descriptive points under the definition, e.g., while we have never used the term ecotourism to market ourselves, I believe by acting responsibly, we are ecotourists.... However, under the strictest guidelines of the WTO definition, we would not qualify. We use local whenever possible, but we have found we must employ residents of the country from which travelers originate, to better interpret cultural & educational issues • feel strongly ecotourism should contribute to the protection of natural areas & support local economies & local conservation efforts • ecotourism should offer an opportunity to participate in a cultural/nature environment with appreciation and not impact.

Tour Operator Focus Groups (15)

- All Montreal participants agreed with the WTO definition of ecotourism. It was considered good to make a distinction between nature, adventure, outdoor and ecotourism experiences.
- The Toronto group also agreed with the WTO definition, but qualified their agreement, by saying it is a very broad description, which is rather all-encompassing, and which may give everyone a reason to use the term in their products.
- There were some comments that such components as "small group" might themselves be subject to abuse (e.g., some see small as being 8-10 people, while others see it as 30).
- Other concerns were that constraining the use of "ecotourism" to "relatively undisturbed areas" is limiting, since many tours now have a rehabilitation component for natural areas, thus while they would benefit the environment and fulfil the intent of the WTO definition on the one hand, ironically, they would not qualify for the definition on the other hand.
- Some operators had a problem not with the definition of ecotourism per se, but with the term "ecotourism" itself. They feel it has become a "label" which is now a problem. They feel the word "sustainable" might be a better term to consider using.

Little Use of the Term "Ecotourism" Among Operators

The majority of tour operators (13 of 23) did not use the term "ecotourism" in the marketing or promotion of their company or products, while 10 use this term. One indicated that while they used the word ecotourism, they preferred to used "ecoadventure tourism".

Focus groups with tour operators revealed that the term "ecotourism" is not used to a large extent. Those who do use the word in their marketing materials, explain it to their clients. Their explanations involve key phrases such as "a trip which respects the environment", or "small groups", etc. It should be noted that the values/elements which the WTO imbues in the term "ecotourism" are often part of many operators' product offerings, it is simply that *operators choose not to use the word ecotourism*.

Operators may use other terms to describe their product, such as "nature tourism" or "sustainable Tourism", or "eco-adventure tourism". The latter term is used because they feel this implies that the visitor experience focuses on adventure, but respects the environment and peoples, and includes a learning experience.

Operators feel that their customers are not highly aware of the differences in meaning of terms such as ecotourism and nature tourism. In addition, they said that there is confusion, even among the tour companies, about the definitions of the words "adventure" and "ecotourism".

Negative Opinions about Use of Term "Ecotourism" Exist with Tour Operators

Many operators revealed an element of reluctance to use the term ecotourism, or even categorical avoidance, because of **the feeling there may be: overuse, abuse, or too much "greenwashing" within the industry**. It is considered "a buzz word" and "marketing gimmick" by some ("*anyone who doesn't drop his or her garbage on the path is termed an ecotourist*").

- **it is industry consensus opinion that while there are many bona fide operators who adhere to the principles of ecotourism and use that term, they feel that most do not**

Other reasons why operators were reluctant to use the word ecotourism include the impression that ecotourism relates only to nature, whereas operators may have a large cultural or heritage component in their products.

An interesting comment by one operator is that "*the word ecotourism has gone through its entire product life cycle and now needs something else*". While this might be an extreme opinion, it is interesting that they view ecotourism as a product, with a life cycle. The operator did not explain this further, although the comment implies that ecotourism is some kind of fad, despite its sustained popularity for more than a decade. However, it may be relevant that of the 22 operators, who indicated they sold ecotourism products according to the WTO definition, half said that they did not use the word ecotourism in marketing their product. There is clearly some tour operator reluctance to use the word ecotourism, and perhaps more research is required on this.

Independent Travellers

Attitudes to the Words Nature Tourism and Ecotourism

In the ecotourism focus group, there seemed to be some degree of understanding of the difference in the terms nature tourism, and ecotourism, by travellers, but not in a clear-cut way. One respondent didn't know the difference between the terms, and another said there was no difference, but other participants (11) gave their opinions. The following chart details these comments and opinions about the differences between the terms nature tourism, and ecotourism:

Focus Group Perceptions of Nature Tourism and Ecotourism

Nature Tourism	Ecotourism
• Trips to specific destinations for the purpose of experiencing and learning about natural history	• I don't know what the word ecotourism means anymore. It means whatever you want it to. Sounds like a marketing strategy
• Involves habitat, birds, flora, fauna, not roughing it	• Avoid using ecotourism
• Both foster an appreciation and respect for nature, and seek to minimize impact caused by human intrusion. But nature tourism involves a trip where the viewing and enjoyment of natural features (mountains, canyons)	• Both foster an appreciation and respect for nature, and seek to minimize impact caused by human intrusion. But ecotourism goes one step further by increasing the tourist's experience via hiking, mountain climbing, rafting, trekking.
• A trip that goes beyond tourist destinations, off trail and away from urban centres with particular attention paid to nature	• Trip in an ecologically sound manner
• Nature tourism would have something to do with seeing nature – like whales, bugs, etc. Nature tourism is a hands on *experience*, with conservation opportunities	• Ecotourism is an idea that would attract the "granola population" – those perceived to rough it
	• Looking at ecosystems of the destinations
• Look at what the places have to offer (historical viewpoints)	• Destinations that offer low environmental impact to surroundings
• Offer travellers a chance to experience nature (and not McDonalds)	• To me the words are interchangeable. To travel to a place with natural or ecological interest
• To me the words are interchangeable. To travel to a place with natural or ecological interest	• *Interpreting* nature and applying it to human lifestyles
• *Looking* at nature	• Changing use of the word. I can mean whatever you want it to mean. It has connotations of roughing it. It sounds like a marketing strategy, and has too much of a "tour" connotation
• "Natural areas" or wildlife safaris	

There were a number of reactions to the term ecotourism, some of them negative. Discussion about ecotourism included:

- Ecotourism doesn't include hunting-based cultures – there would be more of a focus on research

- The terms are misleading: operators use labels to attract tourists

- Even if there are low numbers of people, there still might be high impact

- Environmental and cultural sensitivity are overused, and gimmicky

- Ecotourism in an "in" term, politically correct, with no specific meaning

- If trips are small in scope, they should aim to teach about the local ecosystems including how humans can interact within the systems on a sustainable basis

- Ecotourism suggests more sensitivity toward the environment

- Ecotourism seems to be more adventurous

- Destinations that will provide experiences in the outdoors and nature in its natural state

- Ecotourism is probably more ecosystem friendly in that it offers the least environmental impact

Words Sought by Travellers in the Vacation Description

None of the travellers specifically looked for the word "ecotourism" in the descriptions of the trip they desired. One respondent said "not necessarily". Only one respondent said they looked for the words "nature tourism" in the description of trips. The discussion led quickly into the qualities/words that participants were looking for, including: natural areas, backpacking, having the perception of less impact, desire to support the local community, and needing to do things to support personal principles.

- **Ecotourists were seeking tangible descriptions, rather than "ecotourism" or "nature tourism"**

Appendix B: Canadian Ecotourist Survey Instrument

Ecotourism: Nature - Adventure - Culture Tourism Survey
Alberta-British Columbia, May 1994

Record the following:

interviewer I.D. number _____

date of interview _____

location (city) _____

telephone number ( ) _____

[Ask to speak to a female or male head of household. Try to interview as many males as possible (as close to 50/50 male to female as possible).]

[If not in or available, arrange call back time.]

Hello, I am (both names   ). I am calling you from Alberta, Canada. I'm doing a tourism survey for Alberta and British Columbia in Canada. I am interested in talking to you about vacations you have taken and those you may dream of taking. This will be an interesting survey where you get to talk about your vacation dreams and I hope you have a few minutes to talk to me.

1.a   Have you, or any adult member in your household, taken a vacation out of _____
(mention the state or province you are calling) in the last three years?
(Adult is 18+ years)

yes   1.   **(Ask 1.b and follow pattern)**

no   2.   (Terminate interview)

1.b   Have you, or any adult member of your household, taken a vacation that involved activities related to nature, outdoor adventure, or learning about another culture and which were experienced in the countryside or wilderness?

      yes   1.   (was that yourself? Talk to the member of the household who has taken the vacation type described) **go to 2**.

      no   2.   (ask 1.c and follow pattern)

1.c   Are you interested in taking a vacation where you would experience nature, or outdoor adventure, or learn about another culture?

      yes   1.   **(go to 3)**

      no   2   **(terminate interview)**

2.   For the **last** vacation that you took which included a nature, adventure or cultural experience in the countryside, please answer the following:

2.a   Where did you go?   _____   (location, e.g., Galapagos)

      (don't need to fill all)   _____   (state or province **probe**)

                                   _____   (country)

2.b   On that trip, which activities, events or experiences did you enjoy the most that related to nature, adventure, or culture?

      i.   _____

      ii.   _____

      iii.   _____

      iv.   _____

      v.   _____

2.c   What information sources did you use to find out about and learn about your vacation?
(Prompt, don't read. Circle all responses.)

friends/family _____ 1

books/magazines _____ 2

travel brochure _____ 3

word of mouth _____ 4

travel Association/Bureau _____ 5

personal experience/there before _____ 6

travel Agent _____ 7

T.V. _____ 8

other **(specify)** 9_____

2.d   What were the main reasons you decided to take this trip?
(Probe: What appealed to you the most? Circle all responses.)

visit family and friends _____ 1

rest/relax/get away _____ 2

enjoy the scenery and nature _____ 3

to see the mountains _____ 4

to visit the ocean _____ 5

wildlife viewing (whale watching/other animals/birds/plants/etc.) ___ 6

experience cultural attractions/events/activities _____ 7

new experiences/places to travel _____ 8

to take part in specific land activities (riding/climbing/hiking/cycling/etc.) _____ 9

to take part in specific water activities (cruise/canoeing/kayaking/sailing/etc.) _____ 10

to study to learn about nature/cultures _____ 11

I've been there and want to go again _____ 12

other **(specify)** _____ 13

2.e   Which of the following best describe how you booked this trip? **(Read all choices)**

travel agent ——————————————————————— 1

made my own arrangements/as went along/myself directly —————— 2

club or association ————————————————————— 3

other **(specify)** ———————————————————— 4

2.f   How long before you took the trip did you start planning for it? **(Prompt if necessary)**

0 to 3 months	1	4 to 5 months	2
6 months	3	7 to 11 months	4
1 year	5	between 1 and 2 years	6
2 years	7	more than 2 years	8

2.g   What were the most significant problems, if any, you might have encountered on that trip? **(Circle all responses.)**

none ———————————————————————————— 1

weather ————————————————————————— 2

theft/crime ———————————————————————— 3

nature related (bugs/poor scenery/etc.) ———————————— 4

transportation ———————————————————————— 5

cost ———————————————————————————— 6

health ——————————————————————————— 7

food ———————————————————————————— 8

lodging/hotel/accommodation ——————————————————— 9

Customs/crossing/regulations/duties/taxes ————————————— 10

other **(specify)**——————————————————————— 11

Ask #3 of ALL Respondents

3.a **(For those who responded to #2)** If you were to take another vacation that involved nature, adventure, or learning about another culture in the countryside, what types of activities would you enjoy?

(For those who responded only to #1) What types of vacation activities would you enjoy that involved nature, adventure, or learning about another culture in the countryside?

i. _____

ii. _____

iii. _____

iv. _____

v. _____

3.b Which country, state, or province would appeal to you the most for taking a trip of this type? This can be anywhere you may want to go, a place you might consider going to some time. **(If Canada or U.S. probe province or state. If Alberta or B.C. probe location. Select only first two if more than one.)**

_____ (location, e.g., Galapagos)

_____ (state or province **probe**)

_____ (country)

_____ (location, e.g., Galapagos)

_____ (state or province **probe**)

_____ (country)

3.c   Why is this location and type of trip most appealing to you?

visit family and friends _____ 1

rest/relax/get away _____ 2

enjoy the scenery and nature _____ 3

the wilderness experience _____ 4

to see the mountains _____ 5

to visit the ocean _____ 6

wildlife viewing (whale watching/other animals/birds/plants/etc.) _____ 7

experience cultural attractions/events/activities _____ 8

new experiences/places to travel _____ 9

to take part in specific land activities (riding/climbing/hiking/cycling/etc.) _____ 10

to take part in specific water activities (cruise/canoeing/kayaking/sailing/etc.) _____ 11

to study to learn about nature/cultures _____ 12

I've been there and want to go again _____ 13

other (**specify**) _____ 14

3.d (i) Describe the type of accommodation you think you would choose for this vacation when you are enjoying the nature, outdoor adventure, or cultural experiences. (**Circle all that apply. Record "other", and record all additional comments such as luxury, location, wilderness, etc.**)

hotel/motel _____ 1

lodge/inn _____ 2

cabin _____ 3

tent _____ 4

cruise ship _____ 5

ranch _____ 6

bed & breakfast _____ 7

other (**specify**)_____ 8

Comments _____

_____

_____

(ii)   Which of the following best describes the level of luxury you prefer for this accommodation? (**Read all choices**)

luxurious   1

middle range   2

basic/budget   3

3.e   Which of the following would best describe yourself and the others who might travel with you on this trip? (**Read all choices**)

alone _____ 1

a couple, adults living in the same household _____ 2

myself and a friend not from same household _____ 3

two couples _____ 4

family with adults and children _____ 5

don't know (**don't read this choice**) _____ 6

3.f   In which months of the year do you think you would prefer to take this trip?
(**Circle all responses**)

January	1	July	2
February	2	August	4
March	3	September	6
April	4	October	8
May	5	November	9
June	6	December	10

3.g (i) What is your preference for the total length of this trip you might take?

less than one day	1
1 to 3 days	2
4 to 7 days	3
8 to 14 days	4
more than 14 days	5

(ii) What is your preference for the length of the portion of the trip that will involve nature, culture, or adventure?

less than one day	1
1 to 3 days	2
4 to 7 days	3
8 to 14 days	4
more than 14 days	5

3.h What are the things that concern you the most, that worry you about taking such a vacation?

nothing	1
weather	2
theft/crime/safety	3
nature related (bugs/poor scenery)	4
transportation	5
cost	6
health	7
food	8
lodging/hotel/accommodation	9
Customs/crossing/regulations/duties/taxes	10
other (**specify**)	11

3.i   I would like to read you a list of services and activities you might experience while travelling on this vacation. Please rate how important each one is to you, on a scale of one to five, with 1 the most important and 5 the least important.

i.	a wilderness setting _____	1	2	3	4	5
ii.	visiting a national park or other protected area _____	1	2	3	4	5
iii.	learning about other cultures _____	1	2	3	4	5
iv.	interpretative educational programs _____	1	2	3	4	5
v.	participating in physically challenging activities _____	1	2	3	4	5
vi.	the importance of guides _____	1	2	3	4	5
vii.	viewing wildlife _____	1	2	3	4	5
viii.	mountain cycling _____	1	2	3	4	5
ix.	casual walking _____	1	2	3	4	5
x.	hiking/trekking _____	1	2	3	4	5
xi.	trail riding (horse) _____	1	2	3	4	5
xii.	rafting/canoeing/kayaking on a river or lake _____	1	2	3	4	5
xiii.	cross counry skiing _____	1	2	3	4	5
xiv.	ocean sailing/kayaking _____	1	2	3	4	5
xv.	cycling _____	1	2	3	4	5

4.   Which of the following best describes how much you think you would be prepared to pay and able to afford for this vacation you just described? This is the total amount **per person**, for the total vacation package. This per person cost includes transportation to and from your home, food, accommodation and all other costs for the travel experiences. **(Read choices - have them respond in their currency)**

less than $500 per person	1
$501 to $1,000 per person	2
$1,001 to $1,500	3
$1,501 to $2,000	4
$2,001 to $3,000	5
$3,001 to $5,000	6
over $5,000 per person	7

5.a   Have you ever been on a vacation trip to the province of Alberta in Canada?

        no   1 **(Go to #6.a)**

        yes   2 **(Ask #5.b and follow the pattern)**

5.b   While visiting Alberta did you take part in experiences that involved nature, adventure or learning about another culture?

        no   1 **(Go to #6.a)**

        yes   2 **(Ask #5.c and move on to #6.a)**

5.c   Describe your specific nature, outdoor adventure, and cultural experiences and activities in Alberta.

    i.   _____

    ii. _____

    iii. _____

    iv. _____

    v. _____

6.a   Have you ever been on a vacation trip to the province of British Columbia in Canada?

        no   1 **(Go to #7.a)**

        yes   2 **(Ask #6.b and follow the pattern)**

6.b   While visiting British Columbia did you take part in experiences that involved nature, outdoor adventure, or learning about another culture?

        no   1 **(Go to #7.a)**

        yes   2 **(Ask #6.c and move on to #7.a)**

6.c Describe your specific nature, adventure, culture experiences and activities in British Columbia.

i. _____

ii. _____

iii. _____

iv. _____

v. _____

Ask of ALL Being Interviewed

7.a Would you be interested in coming, or returning to British Columbia or Alberta for a vacation trip such as you've previously described for your "dream" vacation?

no   1

yes   2

7.b What are the barriers, the things that would prevent you from taking such a vacation to British Columbia or Alberta? (Circle all responses.)

money/cost/finances	1
time/work	2
nothing/none	3
family responsibilities	4
lack of knowledge/awareness	5
fear	6
distance	7
not interested	8
other (please specify) _____	9

8. How many vacation pleasure travel trips outside of your state or province have you taken in the last three years? (**Circle the appropriate number**)

0	4
1	5
2	6 or more
3	

9.   Do you do or have you done any of the following?

- belong to nature oriented clubs or organizations?
  no   1
  yes   2   Which?   i. _____
                                           ii. _____

- read any outdoor adventure or nature magazines and publications?
  no   1
  yes   2   Which?   i. _____
                                           ii. _____

[Finally, I'd just like to ask you a couple of questions about yourself.]

10.a   Which of the following best describes your household? **(Read choices)**
        I live alone   1
        I live with another adult   2
        couple with children   3
        single with children   4

10.b   Which of the following best describes your age?
        18 to 24   1
        25 to 34   2
        35 to 44   3
        45 to 54   4
        55 to 64   5
        65 to 74   6
        75 and over   7

10.c   Which of the following best describes the highest level of education you have been able to obtain?
        less than high school   1
        graduated from high school   2
        1 to 3 years of college, university 3
        graduated from college   4

(Record sex of respondent)
        male   1
        female   2

[Your cooperation with this survey has been greatly appreciated.]

(If respondent wishes information on travel in Alberta or British Columbia, toll free numbers are below. A travel counsellor can provide them with information and materials.)

British Columbia   1-800-661-8888
Alberta   1-800-663-6000

Appendix C: Tour Operators Responding to Survey*

Great Canadian Travel Company
158 Fort St. Winnipeg, MBR3C 1C9
Tel: 204 949-0199
Fax: 204 949-0188
Sales@gctc-mst.com
www.greatcanadiantravel.com

Hanover Holiday Tours Ltd.
Ontario
Tel:519 364-4911
Fax: 519 364-2299
Hanhol@log.on.ca
www.hanoverholidays.com

Nahanni River Adventures
Box 31203 Whitehorse, YK Y1A 5P7
Tel: 867-668-3180
Fax: 867-668-3056
Info@nahanni.com
www.nahanni.com

Adventure Network International
4800 N. Federal Hwy. Ste. 307D, Boca Raton,
FL 33431
Tel: 561-237-2359
Fax: 561 347-7523
General@adventure-network.com
www.adventure-network.com

Fresh Tracks Canada
#202 1807 Maritime Mews, Granville Island,
Vancouver, BC V6H 3W7
Tel: 1-604-737-8743 1-800-667-4744
Fax: 1-604-718-5110
adventure@freshtracks.ca
www.freshtracks.ca

Quest Nature Tours
1170 Sheppard Ave. W. Ste. 45, Toronto,
ON M3K 2A3
Tel: 416-633-5666
Fax: 416-633-8667
travel@worldwidequest.com
www.questnaturetours.com

Voyages Loisirs
4545 Pierre-de Coubertin, Montreal,
QC H1V 3R2
Tel: 514 252-3129, 1-800-932-3735
Fax: 514 253 5537
Voyagesloisirs@loisirquebec.qc.ca
www.loisirquebec.qc.ca/voyage

Country Walkers
P.O. Box 180, Waterbury, VT 05676
Tel: (1-800) 464-9255
Fax: 802 244 5661
Info@countrywalkers.com
www.countrywalkers.com

---

*   Note, one respondent is missing, due to request for confidentiality

Worldwide Ecolodges
Ste 503, 4500-39 St. NW, Calgary,
AB T3A 0M5
Tel: 403 288 5328
Fax: 403 247-3218
Wwe@tourworld.ab.ca
www.worldwideecolodges.com

Tours of Exploration
PO Box 48225, Vancouver, BC V7X 1N8
Tel: 1-800-690-7887
Fax: (604) 886-7304
Info@toursexplore.com
www.toursexplore.com

Federation of Ontario Naturalists
355 Lesmill Rd. Don Mills, ON M3B 2W8
Tel: 416 444-8419, 1-800-440-2366
Fax: 416 444-9866
Wfw@ontarionature.org
www.ontarionature.org

Bestway Tours & Safaris
206-8678 Greenall Ave. Burnaby, BC V5J 3M6
Tel 604 264-7378
Fax 604 264-7774
Bestway@bestway.com
www.bestway.com

Toronto Zoo
361A Old Finch Ave., Scarborough,
ON M1B 5K7
Tel: (416) 392-5937
Fax: (416) 392-5948
cgreenla@zoo.metrotor.on.ca
www.torontozoo.org

Évasions S.B.M.
(société de biologie de Montréal)
4777 ave Pierre-de-Coubertin,
Montréal QC H1V 1B3
Tel: 514-868-3278
Fax: 514-868-3065
renerobi@colvir.net
Http://sbm.umontreal.ca

GAP Adventures
19 Duncan St. Ste. 401 Toronto ON M5H 3H1
Tel: 416-260-0999
Fax:416 260 1888
adventure@gap.ca
www.gapadventures.com

Hibiscus Tours International Ltd.
77 High Park Blvd. Ste. 2, Toronto,
ON M6R 1M9
Tel: 416-534-2299
Fax: 416-537-1975
info@hibiscus.ca
www.hibiscus.ca

The Great Canadian Adventure Company
#300 10190-104 Street, Edmonton,
AB T5J 1A7
780 414 1676
780 424 9034
troy@adventures.ca
www.adventures.com

Odyssey Learning Adventures
182 Princess St., Kingston, ON K7L 1B1
Tel: 613 549 3561
Fax: 613 548 1787
Learning@odyssey-travel.com
www.odysseylearningadventures.ca

Karavaniers du monde
9 de la Commune ouest,
Montréal QC H2Y 2C5
Tel: 514-281-0799
Fax: 514-281-5664
expeditions@karavaniers.com
www.karavaniers.com

TBR Plus
34 Flintridge Road, Toronto, ON M1P 1C3
416 701 0756
fax 416 701 0751
tebrplus@hotmail.com
www.travelbyrail.com

SNV International Ltd.
1045 Howe St. #402, Vancouver, BC V7G 2N3
Tel: 604-683-5101
Fax: 604-683-5129
snv@snvgroup.com
www.snvgroup.com

Global Connections
Ste. 408 1199 W. Pender St. Vancouver,
BC V6E 2R1
Tel: 604 681 1221
Fax: 604 681 2754
Glblconx@istar.ca

Elder Treks
597 Markham St. Toronto, ON M6G 2L7
416 588 5000
416 588 9839
gordon@eldertreks.com
www.eldertreks.com

Calgary Zoo,
Botanical Garden & Prehistoric Park
1300 Zoo Road N.E.. Calgary, AB T2E 7V6
Tel: (403) 232-9300
(800) 588-9993
Fax (403) 237-7582
BrianK@calgaryzoo.ab.ca
http://www.calgaryzoo.ab.ca/

Trek Holidays (West Can Treks)
8412-109 Street, Edmonton, AB T6G 1E2
780 939 9118
Fax: 780 433 5494
Allan@trekholidays.com
www.trekholidays.com

EcoRes Travel
#1101– 2001 Beach Avenue,
Vancouver BC V6G 1Z3
Tel: 604 608 9560
Toll Free: 1- 877-532-6737
Fax: 604-608-9560
info@eco-res.com
www.eco-res.com

The Adventure Travel Company
381 King St. W., Toronto, ON
Tel: 416 345-9726
Fax: 416 345-9899
Rruttan@atcadventure.com
www.atcadventure.com

Active Journeys Inc.
4891 Dundas St. W. #4 Toronto, ON M9A 1B2
Tel: 416 236-5011
Fax: 416 236-4790
Info@activejourneys.com
www.activejourneys.com

Appendix D: Tour Operator Focus Group Participants

Toronto and Montreal

Bob Ruttan
THE ADVENTURE TRAVEL COMPANY
381 King St. W., Toronto, ON
Tel: 416 345-9726
Fax: 416 345-9899
Rruttan@atcadventure.com
www.atcadventure.com

Sarah Winterton
FEDERATION OF ONTARIO NATURALISTS
355 Lesmill Rd. Don Mills, ON M3B 2W8
Tel: 416 444-8419, 1-800-440-2366
Fax: 416 444-9866
Wfw@ontarionature.org
www.ontarionature.org

Bruce Poon Tip
GAP Adventures,
19 Duncan St. Ste. 401 Toronto ON M5H 3H1
Tel: 416-260-0999
Fax:416 260 1888
adventure@gap.ca
www.gapadventures.com

Marcus Shalar
Horizon Nature Adventures
4165-A rue st-Denis, Montreal QC H2W 2M7
Tel: 514-286-6010
Toll Free:1-888-318-6010
Fax: 514-286-0179
www.hna.qc.ca
nature@hna.qc.ca

Anne Brobyn
Hibiscus Tours International Ltd.
77 High Park Blvd. Ste. 2, Toronto,
ON M6R 1M9
Tel: 416-534-2299
Fax: 416-537-1975
info@hibiscus.ca
www.hibiscus.ca André Daigle

René Robitaille,
Évasions S.B.M.
(société de biologie de Montréal)
4777 Ave. Pierre-de-Coubertin, Montréal,
QC H1V 1B3
Tel: 514-868-3278
Fax: 514-868-3065
renerobi@colvir.net
Http://sbm.umontreal.ca

Gordon Ross
ELDER TREKS
597 Markham St. Toronto, ON M6G 2L7
416 588 5000
416 588 9839
gordon@eldertreks.com
www.eldertreks.com

Carolyn Greenland
TORONTO ZOO
361A Old Finch Ave., Scarborough,
ON M1B 5K7
Tel: (416) 392-5937
Fax: (416) 392-5948
cgreenla@zoo.metrotor.on.ca
www.torontozoo.org

Pamela Burton
QUEST NATURE TOURS
1170 Sheppard Ave. W. Ste. 45, Toronto,
ON M3K 2A3
Tel: 416-633-5666
Fax: 416-633-8667
travel@worldwidequest.com
www.questnaturetours.com

Hope Burridge
RAZDAN HOLIDAYS
34, Flintridge Road, Toronto, ON MIP 1C3
Tel: 416-701-0756
Fax: 416-701-0751
Toll Free: 1-877-271-4479
travelbyrail@hotmail.com
www.razdanholidays.com/

André Daigle
VOYAGES LOISIRS
4545 Pierre-de Coubertin, Montreal,
QC H1V 3R2
Tel: 514 252-3129, 1-800-932-3735
Fax: 514 253 5537
Voyagesloisirs@loisirquebec.qc.ca
www.loisirquebec.qc.ca/voyage

Richard Remy
Karavaniers du Monde
9, de la Commune West,
Montréal QC H2Y 2C5
Tel: (514) 281-0799
Fax : (514) 281-5664
expeditions@karavaniers.com
www.karavaniers.com

Julien Tasserini
EXPLORATEURS VOYAGES
322, Ontario East, Montréal QC H2X 1H6
Tel: (514) 847-1177
Fax: (514) 847-5323
explorateur@videotron.ca
www.explorateur.qc.ca Pierre Proulx

Éric Morrissette
Zone 0 (virtual company)
destinations@zone0.net
www.zone0.net

Pierre Proulx
PASSION VOYAGE
911, Beaubien East, Suite 1,
Montréal QC H2S 1T2
Tel: 514-279-5317
Fax: 514-279-0998
passion.voyage@videotron.ca
www.er.uqam.ca/nobel/k16305/Voyage/Pas-
sionVoyage.html

Appendix E: Canadian Surveys – Summarised Results of Surveys of Independent Canadian Nature Tourists and Ecotourists*

Socio-Economic Profiles

Market Characteristics	Canada/US Nature/adventure/culture tourists [1] N = 1,384	Canada/(Ontario) Nature Tourists 1994 N=556 [2]	Canada/US (Ontario) Nature Tourists 1994 N=799 [3]	Canadian Ecotourists 1992 [4]	Canadian International Nature Tourists 2000 [5]	Canadian "Purer" Ecotourists 1994 [6] N = 120
Origins	From sampled residents (therefore does not necessarily represent propensity for adventure)	Total intercept 55% US 44% Canadian (30% of which from N. Ontario)	Total mail survey 55% US 43% Canadian (of which most were from S. Ontario)	Sample from Canada, mostly from Ontario	48% Ontario 18% BC 17% Quebec 9% Alberta	From sampled residents in Winnipeg and Toronto
Household Income	Live in neighbourhoods with >US$35,000 (CDN$45,000)	18% <$30,000 39% $30,001-50,000 23% $50,001-70,000 19% >$70,001	21% <$30,000 20% $30,001-50,000 22% $50,001-70,000 **37% >$70,001**	16% <$30,000 25% $30,000-49,999 21% $50,000-69,999 **36% >$70,000** av. ~$64,000 CDN	No information available	Live in neighbourhoods of >$45,000 CDN
Age	10% 18-24 24% 25-34 **25% 35-44** 18% 45-54 23% 55+	9% 20-29 **35% 30-39** 31% 40-49 16% 50-59 13% 60-69 5% 70+ **34% is 50+**	7% 16-20 **28% 20-29** 20% 40-49 20% 40-49 8% 50-59 3% 60-69 1% 70+	3% 15-24 11% 25-34 20% 35-44 **23% 45-54** **23% 55-64** 11% 65-69 11% 70+ **45% is 55+**	9% 0-19 5% 20-24 16% 25-34 **17% 35-44** **23% 45-54** **18% 55-64** 10% 65-74 3% 75+ **31% is 55+**	9% 18-24 **26% 25-34** **18% 35-44** **22% 45-54** 12% 55-64 10% 65-74 3% 75+ **25% 55+**

Market Characteristics	Canada/US Nature/adventure/culture tourists [1] N = 1,384	Canada/(Ontario) Nature Tourists 1994 N=556 [2]	Canada/US (Ontario) Nature Tourists 1994 N=799 [3]	Canadian Ecotourists 1992 [4]	Canadian International Nature Tourists 2000 [5]	Canadian "Purer" Ecotourists 1994 [6] N = 120
Gender	males & females, varies by activity	50:50	65% male 35% female	50:50	Females 57% of travel party, males 43%	Males & females, varies by activity
Household Composition	44% couples 1/3 families	No information	No information	No information	No information	14% alone 44% couples 38% couple w. children 4% single w. children
Education	5% some HS 21% high school 30% some college 45% college grads	13% some high school 16% high school 17% some college 24% college grads	5% some high school 6% high school 65% some college 25% college grads	11% high school or less 24% some post secondary >66% university education	No information	9% some high school 28% high school 26% some college 37% college grads

*Note that due to delays in publication, the dates of the research (in the table headings) may be earlier than the actual dates of publication (in the source materials).

Sources: 1. HLA/ARA 1994 – this includes respondents from 5 US & 2 Canadian cities; 2.Twynam & Robinson 1997 intercept in N. Ontario, Canadian sample only; 3. Twynam & Robinson 1997, Mailback survey, Canadian sample only; 4. Eagles & Cascagnette 1993; 5. Statistics Canada, 2001 – International visitors to parks; 6. Special 2001 runs of 1994 survey focusing on Canadians who are "purer ecotourists" in the sample

Socio-Economic Profiles of Independent Canadian Nature Tourists and Ecotourists

Market Characteristics	Canada/US Nature/adventure/culture tourists [1] N = 1,384	Canada/US (Ontario) Nature Tourists 1994 Intercept N=556 [2]	Canada/US (Ontario) Nature Tourists 1994 Mail N=799 [3]	Canadian International Nature Tourists [4]	Canadian "Purer" Ecotourists 1994 [5] N = 120
Party Composition/ Travelling Companions	59% couples 26% families w. children 7% alone	Future preference 62% family 25% friends & family 11% friends 1% alone org past	Future preference 33% friends 31% family 27% family & friends 3% alone org past	18% alone 50% couple 19% 3 or more adults 1% alone w. children 6% 2 adults w. children 6% 3+ adults w. children 19% 1 person 49% 2 persons 8% 3 persons 13% 4 persons 8% 5-9 persons 3% 10+ persons	5% alone 30% couple 22% couple, different household 5% 2 couples 35% families 3% tour group (57% couples)

Sources: 1. HLA/ ARA 1994 – this includes respondents from 5 US & 2 Canadian cities; 2.Twynam & Robinson 1997 intercept in N. Ontario, Canadian sample only; 3. Twynam & Robinson 1997, Mailback survey, Canadian sample only; 4. Statistics Canada, 2001 – International visitors to parks; 5. Special 2001 runs of 1994 survey focusing on Canadians who are "purer ecotourists" in the sample

Trip Characteristics of Independent Canadian Nature Tourists and Ecotourists

Market Characteristics	Canada/US Nature/ adventure/culture tourists [1] N = 1,384	Canada/US (Ontario) Nature Tourists 1994 Intercept N=556[2]	Canada/US (Ontario) Nature Tourists 1994 Mail N=799[3]	Canadian International Nature Tourists 2000[4]	Canadian "Purer" Ecotourists 1994[5] N = 120
Length of trip Last trip	Whole vs. ecotourism portion of trip 0% <1 day 1% 1-3 days 24% 4-7 days 35% 8-14 days **40% >14 days**	Future preference 7% 1 night 20% 2-3 nights **34% 4-6 nights** 15% 7 nights 24% >7 nights	Future preference 2% 1 night 17% 2-3 nights **42% 4-6 nights** 15% 7 nights 24% >7 nights	0% 1 night 1% 2-3 nights 3% 4-6 nights 29% 7-9 nights 13% 10-13 nights 22% 14-16nights **33% 17+ nights**	Whole (vs. ecotourism portion of) trip 0% <1 day 1% 1-3 days 11% 4-7 days 36% 8-14 days **53% >14 days**
Length of trip Next trip	Whole vs. ecotourism portion of trip 1% <1 day 10% 1-3 days **40% 4-7 days** 27% 8-14 days 23% >14 days				Whole (vs. ecotourism portion of) trip 1% <1 day 6% 1-3 days **36% 4-7 days** 23% 8-14 days 32% >14 days

Sources: 1. HLA/ ARA 1994 – this includes respondents from 5 US & 2 Canadian cities; 2. Twynam & Robinson 1997 intercept in N. Ontario, Canadian sample only; 3. Twynam & Robinson 1997, Mailback survey, Canadian sample only; 4. Statistics Canada, 2001 – International visitors to parks; 5. Special 2001 runs of 1994 survey focusing on Canadians who are "purer ecotourists" in the sample

Destination of Last Ecotourism Vacation

Location of Survey Sample	Ecotourism Destination: Percentage of Respondents						
	Canada	US	Europe	S/C. America	Carib.	Mexico	Other
Total[1]	21 (224)	54 (571)	8 (87)	3 (29)	5 (50)	6 (62)	4 (42)
Canadian Ecotourists	50 (58)	24 (28)	7 (8)	3 (3)	6 (7)	8 (9)	4 (4)

Source: Wight, 2001, reworking unpublished data from HLA/ ARA 1994, differentiating between the North American and the Canadian samples

Preferred Destinations, Reasons for Travel/Destination, and Expenditures

Market Characteristic	North American General Ecotourist (next trip)[1]	Canadian Ecotourists (1994) N = 120 (30.5% of Those interested in nature/adventure/culture)[2]
Preferred Destination	US Sample (970): 21.5% Canada 38.5% US 40% other Canadian sample (384): 64% Canada 12% US 24% other	Last Next Trip 50% 70% Canada 24% 10% US 7% 6% Europe 3% 3% South/Cent. America 6% 2% Caribbean 8% 2% Mexico 4% 7% Other

Sources: 1. HLA/ ARA 1994 – this includes respondents from 5 US & 2 Canadian cities; 2. Special 2001 runs of 1994 survey focusing on Canadians who are "purer ecotourists" in the sample

Main Reasons For Selecting The Vacation Trip

Market Characteristic	North American General Ecotourist (next trip)[1] (multiple responses)	Canadian International Nature Tourists 2000 Statistics Canada - National parks[2]	Canadian Purer Ecotourists (multiple responses) n = 120[3]
Reasons for Destination or main reason for trip	45% scenery 28% new experiences/ place 16% return trip 15% experience cultural attraction 15% see mountains 15% study/learn nature/cultures	63% holiday, vacation 17% visit friend, relatives 8% meetings, trade shows, conventions, seminars 4% other work 3% education study 2% personal	31% rest 31% visit family 17% enjoy scenery 15% new experiences 12% return trip 9% land activities 7% see mountains 6% view wildlife 4% culture attractions 4% water activities

Sources: 1. HLA/ ARA 1994 – this includes respondents from 5 US & 2 Canadian cities; 2. Statistics Canada, 2001 – International visitors to parks; 3. Special 2001 runs of 1994 survey focusing on Canadians who are "purer ecotourists" in the sample

Expenditures and Willingness to Spend

Market Characteristic	Canadian Ecotourists[3]	Canadian International Nature Tourists 2000 Statistics Canada - National Parks Visitors[4]	North American General Ecotourist (next trip)[5] N = 1,384	Canadian Ecotourists (1994) N = 120 (30.5% of Those interested in nature/adventure/culture)[6]
Expenditure / Willingness to Spend/ Person	< $2,000 $2,000-3,999 24.8% $4,000-5,999 24.4% $6,000-7,999 20.5% $8,000-9,999 8.8% $10,000-11,999 4.9% >12,000 10.9%	Expenditures per TRIP < $500 4% $500-999 7% $1,000-1,999 21% $2,000-3,999 30% $4,000-5,999 18% >$6,000 19%	Willingness to spend on total trip < $500 15% $501-1,000 25% $1,001-1,500 21% $1,501-2,000 16% $2,001-3,000 14% $3,001-5,000 6% > $5,000 2%	Willingness to spend on total trip < $500 19% $501-1,000 26% $1,001-1,500 19% $1,501-2,000 14% $2,001-3,000 13% $3,001-5,000 8% > $5,000 3%

Sources: 1. Twynam & Robinson 1997 intercept in N. Ontario, Canadian sample only; 2.Twynam & Robinson 1997, Mailback survey, Canadian sample only; 3. Eagles & Cascagnette 1993; 4. Statistics Canada, 2001 – International visitors to parks; 5. HLA/ ARA 1994 – this includes respondents from 5 US & 2 Canadian cities; 6. Special 2001 runs of 1994 survey focusing on Canadians who are "purer ecotourists" in the sample

Exhibit: Trip Reason and Motivations of Canadian Nature Tourists and Ecotourists

Market Characteristic	North American General Ecotourist (next trip)[1] N = 1,384	Canada/US (Ontario) Nature Tourists 1994 Intercept N=556[2]	Canada/US (Ontario) Nature Tourists 1994 Mail N=7993	Canadian Ecotourists[4]	Canadian International Nature Tourists 2000 Statistics Canada - National parks[5]	Canadian Ecotourists (1994) N = 120 (30.5% of those interested in nature/ adventure/ culture)[6]
Reasons, Motivations	45% scenery & nature 28% new experiences /places 16% been & want to return 15% cultural attraction 15% see mountains 14% study/learn nature & cultures 13% relax & get away from it all	Outcomes Preferred: 1. enjoy scenic beauty 2. enjoy nature 3. do something w. family/friends 4. travel/explore new places 5. relax mentally 6. emotional release from work 7. avoid daily hustle & bustle 8. socialising w. like-minded 9. experience freedom 10. preserving natural env't 11. relax physically 12. learn/appreciate nature 13. preserve forests & wilderness 14. experience new things	Outcomes preferred: 1. enjoy nature 2. enjoy scenic beauty 3. get away from civilization 4. emotional release from work 5. relax mentally 6. experience freedom 7. do something w. family/friends 8. travel/explore new places 9. learn/appreciate nature 10. see maximum in time available 11. socialising w. like-minded 12. avoid daily hustle & bustle 13. preserve natural environment 14. stimulating/exciting experience	1. wilderness/ undisturbed nature 2. learn about nature 3. tropical forests 4. birds 5. photography 6. trees & wildflowers 7. mammals 8. national & provincial parks 9. lakes & streams 10. see maximum in time available 11. mountains 12. oceanside	63% holiday, vacation 17% visit friend, relatives 8% meetings or work 63% holiday, vacation 17% visit friend, relatives 8% meetings or work 4% conventions, trade shows, conferences 3% education study 2% personal	39% scenery 29% new experiences 20% been & want to return 19% see mountains 11% visit family 9% cultural experiences 8% wilderness 7% ocean 6% wildlife viewing 5% water activities 3% study culture 3% land activities

Sources: 1. HLA/ ARA 1994 – this includes respondents from 5 US & 2 Canadian cities; 2 Twynam & Robinson 1997 intercept in N. Ontario, Canadian sample only; 3. Twynam & Robinson 1997, Mailback survey, Canadian sample only; 4. Eagles & Cascagnette 1993; 5. Statistics Canada, 2001 – International visitors to parks; 6. Special 2001 runs of 1994 survey focusing on Canadians who are "purer ecotourists" in the sample

Activity Preferences of Canadian Nature Tourists and Ecotourists

Market Characteristic	North American General Ecotourist (next trip)[1] N = 1,384	Canada/US (Ontario) Nature Tourists 1994 Intercept N=556[2]	Canada/US (Ontario) Nature Tourists 1994 Mail N=799[3]	Canadian International Nature Tourists 2000 Statistics Canada - National parks[4]	Canadian Ecotourists (1994) N = 120 - 30.5% of Those interested in nature/adventure/ culture (last trip)[5]	Canadian Ecotourists (1994) N = 120 - 30.5% of Those interested in nature/adventure/ culture (next trip)[5]
Activity Preferences	**hiking (37%)** touring (20%) camping (19%) boating (17%) walking (17%) fishing (16%) scenery, other than mtn/ocean (14%) swimming (12%) other water (9%) local cultures (8%) cycling (8%)	**Past eco/nature (vs regular) trips to N. Ontario** 21% fishing (vs 20%) 21% camping (vs 11%) 17% sightseeing (vs 30%) 10% hiking (vs 3%) 5% canoeing (vs 4%) **Future Preferred Activities** 1. provincial/nat. parks 2. wildlife viewing 3. waterway parks 4. viewing roadside attractions 5. hiking, day trip 6. interpretation 7. viewing local activities 8. arts & culture 9. native culture 10. swimming	**Past eco/nature (vs regular) trips to N. Ontario** 22% camping (vs 23%) 20% hiking (vs 5%) 17% canoeing (vs23%) 7% fishing (vs 11%) 5% biking (vs 10% sightseeing) **Future Preferred Activities** 1. provincial/nat. parks 2. hiking, daytrip 3. flatwater canoeing, day 4. water parks 5. hiking, multiple daytrips 6. flatwater canoeing, multiple trips 7. wildlife viewing 8. swimming 9. whitewater canoeing 10. interpretation	**Parks & historic sites (100%)** Sightseeing (95%) Shopping (89%) **Zoo, museum, natural display (61%)** Quality dining (55%) Sports/outdoor activities (51%) Nightlife/entertainment (50%) VFR (44%) Swimming (30%) Cultural events (33%) Water sports (20%) Festivals/fairs (19%) Sports (18%) Theme park (13%)	**Walking (24%)** **Hiking (21%)** Camping (20%) Touring (19%) Swimming (16%) Fishing (13%) Scenery other than mtn/ocean (8%) Visiting parks (8%) Skiing (8%)	**Hiking (39%)** **Camping (30%)** Walking (21%) Touring (17%) Swimming (14%) Boating (21%) Fishing (12%) Scenery other than mtn/ocean (12%) Skiing (11%) Cycling (9%) Wildlife viewing (9%) Visiting parks (9%) Local cultures (5%) Rock climbing (5%) Other water activities (3%)

Sources: 1. HLA/ ARA 1994 – this includes respondents from 5 US & 2 Canadian cities; 2.Twynam & Robinson 1997 intercept in N. Ontario, Canadian sample only; 3. Twynam & Robinson 1997, Mailback survey, Canadian sample only; 4. Statistics Canada; 5. Special 2001 runs of 1994 survey focusing on Canadians who are "purer ecotourists" in the sample

Accommodation Preferences of Canadian Nature Tourists and Ecotourists

Market Characteristic	North American General Ecotourist (next trip)[1] N = 1,384	Canada/US (Ontario) Nature Tourists 1994 Intercept N=556[2]	Canada/US (Ontario) Nature Tourists 1994 Mail N=799[3]	Canadian Ecotourists (1994) N = 120 - 30.5% of Those interested in nature/adventure/ culture (last trip)[4]	Canadian Ecotourists (1994) N = 120 - 30.5% of Those interested in nature/ adventure/culture (next trip)[4]
Accommodation	56% hotel/motel 17% camping 14% lodge/Inn 14% cabins 10% B&B 6% friends/relatives 5% RVs 60% mid range luxury 31% basic/budget 9% luxury	Preference 43% motel 16% tent 8% trailer 4% lodge 3% pickup camper	Preference 38% tent 32% motel 7% motel & tent 3% B&B 2% basic lodge	**39% hotel only** **24% combo of types** 11% home of friends or relatives only 8% hotel & home of friends or relatives	**54% hotel/motel** **33% camping** 9% RV 8% lodge/inn 8% cabin B&B 3% Cruise ship 3% House/condo/apt 3% 52% mid range luxury 46% basic budget 2% luxury

Sources: 1. HLA/ ARA 1994 – this includes respondents from 5 US & 2 Canadian cities; 2. Twynam & Robinson 1997 intercept in N. Ontario, Canadian sample only; 3. Twynam & Robinson 1997, Mailback survey, Canadian sample only; 4. Special 2001 runs of 1994 survey focusing on Canadians who are "purer ecotourists" in the sample

Ecotourist Marketing Planning and Information

Market Characteristics	Canada/US Nature/adventure/culture tourists[1] N = 1,384	Canada/US (Ontario) Nature Tourists 1994 Intercept N=556[2]	Canada/US (Ontario) Nature Tourists 1994 Mail N=799[3]	Canadian Ecotourists 1994[4] N = 120
Information Sources Used	**49% Friends or word of mouth** (39%, 10%) 23% personal experience 16% books 14% travel brochure 14% travel association 9% travel agent 2% TV	**71% Word of mouth** 55% tourist office 33% travel magazines 25% magazines in general 22% books 18% newspapers 11% travel agencies 11% travel shows 7% documentaries 7% TV or radio 6% auto club 3% maps	**74% Word of mouth** 45% books 42% tourist office 37% magazines in general 30% travel magazines 14% newspapers 14% travel agencies 8% travel shows 7% documentaries 5% maps 3% TV or radio 3% auto clubs	**38% friends or word of mouth** 22% travel association 19% personal experience 16% travel brochure 15% books 4% travel agent 3% TV

Sources: 1. HLA/ ARA 1994 – this includes respondents from 5 US & 2 Canadian cities; 2.Twynam & Robinson 1997 intercept in N. Ontario, Canadian sample only; 3. Twynam & Robinson 1997, Mailback survey, Canadian sample only; 4. Special 2001 runs of 1994 survey focusing on Canadians who are "purer ecotourists" in the sample

Planning Lead Time

Market Characteristics	Canada/US Nature/ adventure/culture tourists [1] N = 1,384	Canada/US (Ontario) Nature Tourists 1994 Intercept N=556[2]	Canada/US (Ontario) Nature Tourists 1994 Mail N=799[3]	Canadian Ecotourists 1994[4] N = 120
Planning Time	71% 0-3 months 15% 6 months 6% 4-5 months 6% 1 year 2% 7-11 months 1% > 1 year	39% 3-5 months 24% 1-2 months 23% 6-11 months 16% < 1 month 2% > 1 year	36% 3-5 months 30% 1-2 months 19% 6-11 months 12% <1 month 2% > 1 year	72% 0-3 months 12% 6 months 7% 1 year 6% 4-5 months 2% > 1 year 1% 7-11 months

Sources: 1. HLA/ ARA 1994 – this includes respondents from 5 US & 2 Canadian cities; 2.Twynam & Robinson 1997 intercept in N. Ontario, Canadian sample only; 3. Twynam & Robinson 1997, Mailback survey, Canadian sample only; 4. Special 2001 runs of 1994 survey focusing on Canadians who are "purer ecotourists" in the sample

Memberships

Market Characteristics	Canada/US Nature/adventure/culture tourists [1] N = 1,384	Canada/US (Ontario) Nature Tourists 1994 Intercept N=556 [2]	Canada/US (Ontario) Nature Tourists 1994 Mail N=799 [3]	Canadian Ecotourists 1994 [4] N = 120
Memberships	11% members of organsiations 1. Sierra club 2. Other wildlife orgs. 3. Outdoor activity club 4. Fishing/hunting org. 5. Greenpeace	Canadian sample only 13% environmental org/ (US 22%) 9% outdoor org. (US 13%)	Canadian sample only 21% environmental org. (49%) 20% outdoor org. (22%)	**13% members of organisations** 1. Greenpeace 2. National Wildlife Federation 3. Fishing/hunting org. 4. Other wildlife orgs.

Sources: 1. HLA/ ARA 1994 – this includes respondents from 5 US & 2 Canadian cities; 2.Twynam & Robinson 1997 intercept in N. Ontario, Canadian sample only; 3. Twynam & Robinson 1997, Mailback survey, Canadian sample only; 4. Special 2001 runs of 1994 survey focusing on Canadians who are "purer ecotourists" in the sample

Publications

Market Characteristics	Canada/US Nature/ adventure/culture tourists 1 N = 1,384	Canadian Ecotourists 19942 N = 120
Publications Read	61% read publications 1. National Geographic (35%) 2. Outdoor Life 3. Club publications 4. Fishing/hunting 5. General nature 6. General travel 7. General activity/sports	55% read publications 1. National Geographic (39%) 2. Fishing/hunting 3. General nature 4. Canadian Geographic 5. General activity/sports 6. Field & Stream

Sources: 1. HLA/ ARA 1994 – this includes respondents from 5 US & 2 Canadian cities; 2. Special 2001 runs of 1994 survey focusing on Canadians who are "purer ecotourists" in the sample

Appendix F:
Tour Operator Survey

WTO Survey of Canadian Nature and Ecotourism Markets

Tour Operators Survey

The year 2002 is the International Year of Ecotourism. As part of this event, the World Tourism Organisation (WTO) wants to provide information (particularly to receptive destinations) about what makes a destination attractive and of interest to international tour operators and their ecotourism markets. Pam Wight & Associates has been commissioned to examine Canadian ecotourists.

By assisting us with this survey, you will be ensuring that more destinations become aware of your own company's needs and preferences.

We are also willing to share the results of this survey with you.

Note that all your responses will be *strictly confidential* (results will be aggregated).

Your Company

Name of Company: _____

Address: _____

Tel:Fax: _____

Email: Website: _____

Name and Title of survey respondent: _____

Do you wish the name of your company to appear in the appendix of the report,

to increase your visibility in the market? _____ **Yes** _____ **No**

Your Views on Nature Tourism and Ecotourism

1. Do you use the term "ecotourism" in the marketing or promotion of your company or your products?

❑ Yes

❑ No

The following summarises the WTO definitions for nature tourism and ecotourism:

Nature Tourism

*"All types of tourism based on nature where the primary motivation of tourists is the **observation and appreciation of nature**, as well as cultures".*

Ecotourism

*"Ecotourism goes beyond nature tourism, and occurs in relatively undisturbed natural areas, for the main purpose of admiring them and learning more about them. Ecotourism **implies that the tour operator and the visitors will have some responsibility towards the destination, reducing or avoiding impacts on the areas visited**. Ecotourism should **contribute to conservation** of the natural areas, and **contribute local economic benefits**, as well as generating awareness of conservation among residents and visitors."*

In practical terms, ecotourism products should consist of the following:

e. Include educational or interpretative aspects related to nature
f. Consist of small groups
g. Minimise negative impacts on the natural and cultural environments
h. Contribute to the protection of natural areas by:
  • generating economic benefit for locals;
  • employing locally;
  • increasing locals/visitors awareness of the need for environmental and cultural protection.

2. Do you agree with the definition of ecotourism developed by the WTO?

❑ Completely agree
❑ Not really in agreement
❑ Don't agree at all

Could you explain your response? _____

_____

Your Destinations

3. What is the approximate percentage of your ecotourism/nature tourism products sold in the following destinations?

Canada _____ % of eco/nature tourism products sold

US/Mexico _____ % of eco/nature tourism products sold

International _____ % of eco/nature tourism products sold

International *(Please identify the countries or locations)*

❑   Central America: _____

❑   Caribbean: _____

❑   Latin America: _____

❑   Africa: _____

❑   Asia-Pacific: _____

❑   Europe: _____

❑   Other: _____

Length of Vacation

4. On average, how long is the ecotourism/nature tourism vacation that you provide?

Less than one week   ❑

1 week   ❑

1-2 weeks   ❑

2-3 weeks   ❑

over 3 weeks   ❑

5. Is the ecotourism/nature tourism package:

❑ usually a stand-alone package, or _____ %

❑ part of a more general vacation _____ %

6. **Seasonal distribution?**

Spring _____ %   Summer _____ %   Fall _____ %   Winter _____ %

Average Cost of Trip

7. On average, approximately how much would a week's ecotourism/nature tourism package cost per person (*total costs to client, including transportation, accommodation, meals, and daily activities*)?

❑ < $1,000 per person
❑ $1,001 - $1,500
❑ $1,501 - $2,000
❑ $2,001 - $3,000
❑ $3,001 - $5,000
❑ > $5,000 per person

The Relative Importance of Nature Tourism and Ecotourism to your Operations

8. Using the WTO definitions:

• what proportion of your activities would you say were "nature tourism"? ....%

• what proportion of your activities would you say was "ecotourism"? ....%

9. How do you see the future of the nature and ecotourism markets?

For your company as a whole

In your Canadian markets

❑ Growing   ❑ Growing
❑ Staying the same   ❑ Staying the same
❑ Declining   ❑ Declining

10. What has been your company's turnover in the last 3 years, with respect to:

Total product offerings

Nature & Ecotourism Products

❏ Growing   ❏ Growing

❏ Staying the same   ❏ Staying the same

❏ Declining   ❏ Declining

Average growth/year: _____ %   Average growth/year: _____ %
(over the last 3-5 years)   *(over the last 3-5 years)*

Approximate current numbers of clients _____

Approximate current numbers of clients _____

Your Markets

11. Can you give a general idea of the characteristics of those interested in ecotourism/nature tourism?

Age: *(Provide a rough %)*
❏ 18-24 years _____ %
❏ 25-34 years _____ %
❏ 35-44 _____ %
❏ 45-54 _____ %
❏ 55-64 years _____ %
❏ 65-74 _____ %
❏ 75 and over _____ %

Gender: *(Provide a rough %)*   Male _____ %   Female _____ %

Canadian Origins: *(Provide a rough %)*
❏ Ontario _____ %
❏ Eastern Canada _____ %
❏ Western/Northern Canada _____ %

Party Composition: *(Provide a rough %)*
❏ Singles _____ %
❏ Couples _____ %
❏ Families _____ %
❏ Other _____ %

12. For each of the following, please estimate the importance for your clients taking an ecotourism/nature tourism trip? *(rank each response on a scale of 1-5, with 1 being least important, and 5 being most important)*

☐ Experiencing wilderness/remote areas	1	2	3	4	5
☐ Experiencing parks/protected areas	1	2	3	4	5
☐ Interpretive/learning experience	1	2	3	4	5
☐ Knowledgeable Guides	1	2	3	4	5
☐ Wildlife viewing	1	2	3	4	5
☐ Interacting with aboriginal cultures	1	2	3	4	5
☐ Discovering local cultures and foods	1	2	3	4	5
☐ Contributing to conservation	1	2	3	4	5
☐ Contributing to local community development	1	2	3	4	5
☐ Outdoor activities	1	2	3	4	5
☐ Rest and relaxation in natural settings	1	2	3	4	5
☐ Discovering the exotic	1	2	3	4	5
☐ Socialising with interesting people	1	2	3	4	5
☐ Luxury accommodation	1	2	3	4	5
☐ Other (specify) _____					

13. From your perspective, what are the most important amenities, services, and strengths required at (current or new) destinations, to attract you to package product for ecotourists? *(please specify and describe)*

a) _____

b) _____

c) _____

d) _____

14. For specialised nature/ecotourism product with smaller volumes, what would you say are the preferred types of accommodation and levels of luxury? *(please provide a rough percentage)*

Luxury/semi-luxury Hotel/motel _____ %

Normal hotel/Lodge/inn _____ %

Self-catering Cabin _____ %

Tent/hammock _____ %

Cruise ship _____ %

Bed & breakfast _____ %

Other *(please specify)* _____ % _____

Communication Channels

15. What are you most important methods for you to reach eco/nature tourism clients? *(please rank on a scale of 1-5, with 1 being least important, and 5 being most important)*

Advertisements in specialised magazines	1	2	3	4	5
Media releases	1	2	3	4	5
Trade shows	1	2	3	4	5
Special eco/nature brochures	1	2	3	4	5
Specific messages within your general brochures	1	2	3	4	5
Internet site	1	2	3	4	5
Word of mouth	1	2	3	4	5
Target mailings	1	2	3	4	5
Newsletters	1	2	3	4	5
Travel Agents	1	2	3	4	5

Other *(please specify)* _____

16. What types of information do you provide your ecotourism/nature tourism clients?

❑ Pre-trip information: e.g., list of clothing, equipment, reading materials, etc.

❑ Information meetings/briefings before the trip

❑ Guidelines for conduct, or code of ethics for travellers

❑ Detailed information about habitats, species, ecosystems visited

❑ Information about cultural traditions, the local context for species protection, conservation programs, Non-Governmental organisations who accept donations for these purposes

❑ Other *(please describe)* _____

_____

Support for the Destination

17. Do you encourage your clients to donate to conservation, local development, or community projects?

❑ No

❑ Yes. If yes, do they react favourably? _____ Yes _____ No

18. What kinds of activities do you support at the destination?

❑ Priority given to hiring locally owned/managed operations (guides, accommodation, etc.)

❑ Partner with local operators (receptive operators, lodges, transportation, etc.)

❑ Environmental conservation (through recycling, waste management, conservation of water and energy, etc.)

❑ Partner with protected areas

❑ Supporting local development projects (environmental or community)

❑ Support scientific/research programs

❑ Other (Specify). _____

_____

19. What degree of involvement would you say your eco/nature tourism **clients** have in the following?

Contribute to a nature conservation or protection project
(giving money, etc.) ....%

Participate in a vacation where they donate their time or knowledge
or skills to a project ....%

If you have any other further comments you would like to make, we would love to hear them:

_____

_____

_____

We are interested in your ecotourism/nature products.
Please mail relevant brochures to:
Pam Wight & Associates
14715-82 Ave,
Edmonton,
AB T5R 3R7

Many thanks for your assistance and for your time.